To: _____

Do not be anxious about anything, but in everything, by prayer
and petition, with thanksgiving, present your requests to God.
And the peace of God, which transcends all understanding,
will guard your hearts and your minds in Christ Jesus.

PHILIPPIANS 4:6–7

From: _____

Prayers from a Mom's Heart

Copyright © 2003 by Fern Nichols
ISBN 0-310-98474-2

All Scripture quotations, unless otherwise noted, are taken from the *Holy Bible: New International Version*, (North American Edition). Copyright © 1973, 1978, 1984, by International Bible Society. Used by permission of Zondervan. All rights reserved.

The "NIV" and "New International Version" trademarks are registered in the United States Patent and Trademark Office by International Bible Society.

Requests for information should be addressed to:
Inspirio, The gift group of Zondervan
Grand Rapids, Michigan 49530
http://www.inspiriogifts.com

Published in association with the literary agency of Ann Spangler & Associates, 1420 Pontiac Rd., S.E.
Grand Rapids, MI 49506

Written by: Fern Nichols
Editor: Janice Jacobson
Design Manager: Amy J. Wenger
Design: The Office of Bill Chiaravalle, DeAnna Pierce | www.officeofbc.com

Printed in China
03 04 05/HK/ 4 3 2 1

Prayers

FROM A

Mom's Heart

BY Fern Nichols

inspirio™

Contents

Dear Mom,

It is not easy raising children these days, is it? So many influences and ideas fight for their hearts. I know; I have four children of my own. In the whirlwind of raising children, I have found that prayer is my firm foundation when things around me seemed to be crumbling. Talking with my Heavenly Father gives me hope when I feel hopeless, peace when I am fearful, and wisdom when I don't know what to do. Jesus words, "Come to me all you who are weary and burdened, and I will give you rest" are a promise that I count on. I have experienced a loving, faithful God who hears and answers my prayers.

I am so glad that you are reading this book, for I truly believe that learning how to pray the four prayers of praise, confession, thanksgiving and intercession will change your life. You will come to know who your God is through praise and be strengthened in the conviction that He is able to meet every need that you bring to him. I will share more about the elements of the prayers in the "How to Use This Prayer Guide" section. Each prayer topic will give you sample prayers as well as additional thoughts and Scriptures to use as a springboard for further prayer, privately or in a group, such as Moms In Touch (see page 165 for more information). I have also included stories from moms, just like you, that relate to each topic. They will touch your heart, inspire and encourage you, and let you know that you are not alone in this most challenging and rewarding job of raising children.

My prayer for you, dear mom, is that you will know the joy of an intimate relationship with your Heavenly Father through prayer. He longs for you to talk to him. He says, "Call to me and I will answer you and show you great and mighty things you do not know." There is no prayer too small or too big that God will not hear. Prayer will change things! You will never regret the time that you invest in prayer. It is a legacy that you can give your children that will last forever.

May God bless you and your children,

Fern Nichols

How to Use this Prayer Guide

Most of us would agree with the old saying that "a mother's work is never done." But important as that work is, there is yet something more important, something that has the power to affect our children in the deepest possible way. That something is prayer. When we place our children in God's hands through the power of prayer, we call forth God's blessing and protection. Prayer is not only a wonderful gift to give our children, it is also a powerful antidote to the worry that often accompanies motherhood.

This book will guide and encourage you to pray using four simple prayers: Praise, Confession, Thanksgiving and Intercession. These four steps will transform your relationship with your Heavenly Father, moving you toward greater intimacy and trust. The more you get to know God through prayer and his word, the more you will trust him with everything in your life. This in turn will bring joy, peace and hope to your heart as you pray for your children. God will be faithful to hear and answer your prayers. Sometimes he will say "yes," sometimes "no" and sometimes "wait"—but he will always answer. Because of God's perfect love for you, you can trust that his answers are always best.

I've focused each day's prayer as though your child is asking you to pray directly for a particular need. Though we know that our children may seldom be able to express their need for prayer directly, we also know them well enough to recognize their spiritual, emotional, and physical needs.

The first three steps of each day's prayer—praise, confession and thanksgiving—are for you, Mom. Once you follow these steps your heart will be better prepared to pray with confidence for your child during the intercession time. I am excited for your prayer journey—I know these prayers have the power to revolutionize your life and the lives of your children.

Praise

Each day start with the prayer of praise. This time focuses on one of God's attributes. An attribute is something that is true about God. Each day you will focus on one aspect of God's character. As you get to know God through praising him, you will begin to view your circumstances through the character of God rather than through your own situation. Your eyes will shift from the problem to the problem solver. God knows that it is good for us to put on the "garment of praise instead of a spirit of despair" (Isaiah 61:3). Truly there is no greater way to bring glory to God than to esteem him with your words of praise. As you praise God you will experience a wonderful awareness of his presence.

Confession

Following your time of praise comes a time of confession. Ask God the Holy Spirit to reveal to you any area of your life that may not be pleasing to him. This prayer is very important and requires that you be completely honest before God. If we knowingly hold on to sin in our lives, we block our communication and fellowship with God. Our relationship must be right with God, and with others, if we desire him to hear and answer our prayers.

Therefore, with a humble heart, tell God you are sorry. Do not depend on your feelings to tell you whether you have been forgiven. If you have asked for forgiveness with a sincere heart, then God has forgiven you (1 John 1:9). God always keeps his promise.

Thanksgiving

The third step is to offer a prayer of thanksgiving, expressing appreciation and gratefulness for God's answers. During this time, do not ask God for anything; only offer him your thanksgiving. The apostle Paul tells us in the Bible that we are to give thanks in all things (1 Thessalonians 5:18). When this command is obeyed, it will produce an attitude of gratitude. Even if the answer to your prayer is contrary to what you asked, your thanksgiving expresses confidence in God's plan, crowding out fear and discouragement. Remember that you are not thanking God for difficult circumstances, but you are thanking him for being with you in the midst of them. The benefit of giving thanks is priceless—God's rest!

Intercession

The fourth step can be a powerful time as you come to the Father with boldness to intercede for the needs of your children. Simply stated, an intercessor is one who comes before God to obtain help for someone who is in need. An intercessor does not give up until the answer comes. During this time of praying for your child's specific needs, a Scripture will be given. You may place your child's name right in the verse. By doing this you are praying God's will for him or her. This practice will bring certainty and hope to your heart, increasing your faith as you trust God's promise that his word will not come back empty, but will achieve his great purpose for your child's life (Isaiah 55:10–11).

Mom, no matter what difficulties you or your children may face, you can be confident that your prayers will make a difference!

How to Know That God Will Hear Your Prayers

Just as a mom recognizes the voice of her own child, so the Heavenly Father knows the voice of each one of his children. If you have a question or doubt concerning your relationship with God, let me share with you how you can be certain you are his child.

Think about this unshakable truth: God loves you personally! In his great love he gave the world his greatest treasure—his only child, Jesus Christ. Jesus died on the cross in your place as payment for your sins and for the sins of the whole world. Because of his death and resurrection you can experience God's indescribable love, both now and throughout all eternity.

No matter where your sins have taken you, God's forgiveness is perfect and complete because of the sacrifice of his Son. Will you take your first step of faith by believing in your heart that Jesus died for you? If you accept him into your life as Savior and Lord, you will never be the same. He will replace your loneliness, fears, frustrations and guilt with his love and forgiveness. He also promises to hear your prayers and answer them with all the delight of an earthly parent responding to the desires of a much-loved child.

Make the following prayer the first and most important prayer of your life as you begin praying for your children:

Dear Father, thank you for sending your Son
Jesus to die on the cross for my sin.
I want to be your child.
Please come into my heart and forgive me of all my sins.
I want to live for you alone.
Thank you for making my heart your home.
In Jesus name, Amen.

GOD'S PROMISE TO YOU

To all who receive Jesus, to those who believe in his name,
God gave the right to become children of God.

JOHN 1:12

If you have prayed this prayer you are a member of God's family. You are His child! You now can know for sure that God will hear and answer your prayers.

Welcome to the Family of God.

Mom, I Need to Know God Loves Me

PRAISE GOD BECAUSE HE IS LOVE

God so loved the world that he gave his one and only son,
that whoever believes in him shall not perish but have eternal life.

JOHN 3:16

Heavenly Father, I praise you that you are a God who is love.
There is no love so gracious and measureless as the sacrificial love
that you showed in sending your Son to die for the sins of the whole world.
Though I will never fully understand that kind of selfless love,
my heart rejoices and I will be forever grateful.

CONTINUED PRAISE

God's love is indestructible (ROMANS 8:38–39).
God's love is forever (PSALM 106:1).
God's love is forgiving (PSALM 103:10–12).
God's love is faithful (PSALM 89:24).

CONFESSION

If we confess our sins,
God is faithful and just
and will forgive us our sins
and purify us from all unrighteousness.

1 JOHN 1:9

Dear Father, I ask you to forgive me
for the times I have doubted your love.
Please forgive me when I withhold your love
from others and wound their spirits.
I am so sorry.
Thank you for forgiving me.

REFLECTION: Continue in an attitude of repentance, asking the Holy Spirit to reveal anything that may be blocking your relationship with your Heavenly Father. He is faithful and will cleanse you and will make you new.

Thanksgiving

I will give you thanks, O Lord, for you answered me;
you have become my salvation.

Psalm 118:21

Loving Father, thank you for loving my child
regardless of what he has done or will do.
Thank you for your unchanging love
that knows no boundaries.
I am so grateful that you are always reaching out
with your saving love.

Continued Thanks

Give thanks for the things you love about your child and also for the things that cause you to struggle. Thank God for others who reach out in love to your child, and for the love your child gives you.

Intercession

God demonstrates his own love for us in this:
While we were still sinners, Christ died for us.

ROMANS 5:8

Lord, I ask that my child will experience your unconditional love and realize that he is a sinner and needs a Savior. I pray he will know how deep and wide, how strong and enduring is your personal love for him. May he know complete forgiveness—that there is nothing he could ever do that would take your love from him. May he find his greatest joy and fulfillment in your love. Help him to see that your love is changeless and eternal. In Jesus' name, Amen.

REFLECTION: God's love for your children can satisfy their basic needs for self worth. Does each of your children have a personal relationship with the God who loves them? In what ways can you show them God's love?

Continued Intercession

Pray that your child will love the Lord with all his heart (MARK 12:30).
Pray that he embraces God's love in forgiveness of sin (EPHESIANS 1:7).
Pray that he experiences God's love that casts out fear (1 JOHN 4:18).

God's Promise for Your Child

"I loved the world so much that I gave my one and only Son so that if your child believes in him he shall not perish but have eternal life."

1 JOHN 3: 1, AUTHOR'S PARAPHRASE

THE INTERRUPTION

All three boys were read to, prayed for, kissed and tucked safely into bed. It had been a long day and I was looking forward to a few moments of peace. Retreating to the living room, I turned on the television, flipping the channel to the Billy Graham Crusade. But all too soon I heard the sound of little feet shuffling across shag carpet as my seven-year old son, Troy, began descending the stairs. "Mom, can I have a drink of water?" I motioned him into the living room, wishing he had mentioned his thirst before I tucked him in. Troy sat happily in front of the television while I went to the kitchen to retrieve a glass of water.

Then the phone rang. Another interruption. The call took longer than I'd hoped, and I heard the familiar peals of the Crusade choir singing their final song "Just As I Am" as I walked back into the living room. As I held the glass of water out to Troy, he looked up at me with pensive eyes. "Mom, I want to ask Jesus into my heart right now. Can I?"

"Of course you can." Together we knelt by the sofa, and Troy's voice lifted up a short prayer that must have caused great rejoicing in heaven.

Now many years later, I don't remember who I talked to or what we talked about, but I will never forget that what I thought of as an interruption was the moment God used to reveal his love to Troy. Jesus doesn't need extraordinary moments to carry out his plans for our children. He is more than able to work through the ordinary moments, even the interruptions, to accomplish his purposes. Troy only wanted a drink of water—instead he got a Savior.

Mom, I Need God's Forgiveness

PRAISE GOD BECAUSE HE FORGIVES

In Jesus we have redemption through his blood,
the forgiveness of sins.

EPHESIANS 1:7

Lord, I want to bless you with praise for your gift of forgiveness
given through the death and resurrection of your Son, Jesus Christ.
Your marvelous love has set me free from the guilt
and consequences of my sin. Because you are loving, you are forgiving.
I rejoice and am humbled by your abundant forgiveness.

CONTINUED PRAISE

God's forgiveness is immediate (1 JOHN 1:9).
God's forgiveness is complete (PSALM 85:2).
God's forgiveness is for the undeserving (ROMANS 5:8).
God's forgiveness keeps no record of past sin (PSALM 130:3–4).
God's forgiveness is boundless (PSALM 103:8).

19

CONFESSION

He who conceals his sins does not prosper,
but whoever confesses and renounces them finds mercy.

PROVERBS 28:13

Forgiving Father, sometimes I feel so ashamed of the things I do that I try to hide from you. I move away from you instead of toward you. Forgive me for believing that you are angry with me and that you won't forgive me. I am so sorry for refusing your forgiveness.

REFLECTION: Why is it hard to forgive yourself? Are you tying to hide from God? God promises to forgive you of your sin when you go to him, openly and honestly. Let God's forgiveness sink down deep into your soul, healing you once and for all.

Thanksgiving

As high as the heavens are above the earth,
so great is God's love for those who fear him;
as far as the east is from the west,
so far has he removed our transgressions from us.

PSALM 103:11–12

Lord, I am extremely grateful that I can trust your promise
that you have removed my sins as far away from me
as the east is from the west—
including the guilt and the penalty.
My God, I am forever grateful that you took my sin from me
and placed it on your Son.
When I ask forgiveness, you immediately forgive
and never bring up the offense again.
Your forgiveness is full of love and mercy.
I rejoice in your forgiving heart.

Continued Thanks

Thank God for those you have wronged and do not hold a grudge. Rejoice when your children immediately forgive you when you ask them.

INTERCESSION

There is now no condemnation for those who are in Christ Jesus.

ROMANS 8:1

My Father, I ask that my child will know and experience this truth: that there is now no condemnation for my child because she is in Christ Jesus. I pray she will know, beyond a shadow of doubt that all her sin was paid for by Jesus at the cross. May she not hesitate to come to you in confession and repentance. Touch her heart to understand how much your unconditional love completely forgives. If she is weighted down with guilt, I pray that this truth will penetrate her heart: If she has truly repented of her sin, she is forgiven no matter how she feels. And Lord, please help her to forgive herself. In Jesus' name, Amen.

CONTINUED INTERCESSION

Pray your child accepts Gods forgiveness through his son, Jesus (ROMANS 3:22–24).
Pray your child humbles herself and asks for forgiveness (PSALM 149:4).
Pray your child knows that ALL her sin is forgiven (COLOSSIANS 2:13–14).
Ask God to free your child from guilt (PSALM 32:5).

GOD'S PROMISE FOR YOUR CHILD

If your child has accepted Christ into her heart—
God has rescued your child from the power of darkness and brought her into the kingdom of his Son, whom he loves.
Through Jesus your child has redemption, the forgiveness of sins.

COLOSSIANS 1:13–14, AUTHOR'S PARAPHRASE

EARTHQUAKES

Sometimes life just doesn't work the way we plan. We certainly weren't prepared for the impact that rocked us when our 15-year-old daughter dropped out of school and left home to live with a boy she hardly knew. The four years that followed were painful aftershocks, each tremor dislodging dreams and scattering fragments of all we had hoped for our beautiful daughter's future. She traded her lovely home and loving family for a two-bedroom shack shared by eight occupants located in a questionable section of the city.

Her flare for independence was cramped by debilitating panic attacks. Wanting to provide respite for her to recover, we opened our home and welcomed back the child of our hearts. As she began to evaluate the direction of her life, our daughter returned to school. I smile even now as I recall her graduation: a scene we had at one time erased from our list of dreams for her. Hesitantly, we began to hope and dream the ground was settling under our spirited child.

Unfortunately, our daughter returned to a careless lifestyle, became pregnant and had no health insurance. I cried out to the Lord and pleaded that my daughter would not terminate the life in her womb. The Lord heard the cries of this heart-broken mom—soon to become a grandma!

Shortly after the birth of my beautiful grandchild, the baby's father proposed to my daughter and they began preparing to make their union legal before God and man. How my heart sang with the news!

The flurry of wedding plans shook the ground again, but these were tremors full of joyful anticipation. It was in the dressing room of a wedding boutique that I caught my daughter's reflection in the mirror for one split second, and I could read her mind, Mom, do you forgive me?

Returning my gaze to her image in the mirror, I watched her with the eyes of love. Her radiant face was a permanent fixture in my mind, but in that moment, I really saw her! Dressed in satin and silk, loved and accepted—pure and forgiven.

Mom, I Want to Trust God with My Problems

PRAISE GOD BECAUSE HE IS GOOD

Praise the LORD, for the LORD is good; sing praise to his name, for that is pleasant.

PSALM 135:3

My God, I know that goodness cannot be found apart from you and your ways. Your character is absolutely pure and morally excellent. All you are and all that you do is good. Your goodness is the reason for your compassion, kindness, and generosity. Your goodness never changes and never varies in its intensity. My heart sings your praises for your ability to turn the dark clouds in my life to beautiful sunshine and brilliant blue skies. In your goodness I will hope. God's forgiveness is immediate (1 John 1:9).

CONTINUED PRAISE:

Praise God that everything he created and everything that he does is good
(GENESIS 1:31; PSALM 119:68).

God's goodness is abundant (PSALM 145:4, 7).

God's great goodness is for eternity (PSALM 23:6).

Praise God for the hope his goodness gives to you (PSALM 27:13).

Confession

Who is a God like you,
who pardons sin
and forgives the transgression
of the remnant of his inheritance?
You do not stay angry forever
but delight to show mercy.

MICAH 7:18

Dear Lord, forgive me for not trusting you when I am in crisis.
In those moments I find myself feeling frustrated,
angry, or scared, I forget you are a good God and everything
you allow to happen in my life is for a purpose.
Forgive me for allowing my problems to control my thoughts
and actions instead of trusting in your goodness for me.

REFLECTION: What keeps you from believing with unshake-
able certainty that God is absolutely and completely good to you?
Meditate on the characteristic of God's goodness and let this truth
sink deeply into your soul.

Thanksgiving

Give thanks to the LORD, for he is good;
his love endures forever.

PSALM 107:1

Dear Father, I offer my sincere thanks
that you are a Father who is always good.
You express your goodness in so many loving ways:
to the frightened, you are friendly. To the weak, you are gentle.
To the suffering, you are comfort. To the distressed, you are rest.
To the lonely, you are love. To the lost, you are the way.
To the discouraged, you are hope. To the guilty, you are forgiving.
How I rejoice in the goodness of the Lord.

CONTINUED THANKS

Quiet your heart and consider God's goodness to you and your family, friends, church, home and children. Give thanks for each one. Can you think of a time when God brought good out of a hard circumstance? Have you thanked him?

INTERCESSION

The LORD is good, a refuge in time of trouble.
He cares for those who trust in him.

NAHUM 1:7

My Good God, I pray that my child will believe you are good and a refuge in times of trouble. She is having a hard time and is trying to handle her problems all on her own. I pray that she will not be afraid to relinquish control and give her desires and expectations to you. May my child believe your promise that no matter what the problem is, even the ones she creates herself, everything will work out for her best good. Please help her to trust you completely, so her heart can once again be joyful. In Jesus' name, Amen.

CONTINUED INTERCESSION

Pray for your child to trust God's deliverance (ISAIAH 43:1–2).
Pray for her to trust God's plan for her life (JEREMIAH 29:11).
Pray that she will acknowledge God in all his ways (PROVERBS 3:5–6).
Pray for your child to trust in the promises of God (JOSHUA 23:14).
Ask God to give your child his peace (ISAIAH 26:3–4)

GOD'S PROMISE FOR YOUR CHILD

May your child be confident of this:
that she will see the goodness of the LORD in the land of the living.

PSALM 27:13, AUTHOR'S PARAPHRASE

It's Gone!

My sweet daughter Abby skipped through her childhood losing barrettes, books, and crayons wherever she went. The things she lost, for the most part, were insignificant until her junior year at Texas A & M. Scurrying across campus after volleyball class, she fastened her watch back on and pushed her engagement ring past her slight knuckle. It was not until the middle of her next class that she realized the watch was on but the ring was GONE. She frantically retraced her steps, looking for the glimmer of a gem in the grass. But nothing sparkled and Abby's heart sank.

Tearfully, Abby called home and told us about her loss. Abby assured us that she had placed an ad in the school newspaper hoping that an honest student would find her treasure. Her voice became calmer when I reminded her that Moms In Touch met tomorrow, and we would intercede for her. She and I agreed that this was the Lord's problem now, and we needed to pray … and wait.

The next day my prayer partners joined me in asking that the lost ring would be found by someone with integrity. Later that very evening, Abby received a call. A young man explained that he'd found the ring. He went on to say that he picked up a copy of the school newspaper (something he rarely read) because of an interesting article on the front cover. As he was reading, he remembered the lost ring and scanned the newspaper to see if someone had reported it missing.

When Abby heard the news she squealed with delight and informed him that she was minus one engagement ring! The honest and thoughtful student returned the cherished band to a grateful young woman. He didn't want the reward; he was just glad to help. We consider him a flesh-and-blood example of God's good hand extended!

This may not be the last time Abby loses something, but she has promised to work harder at not being so careless with her possessions. But this incident will always remind Abby that God is good and he is in the business of finding what is lost.

Mom, I Want to Know God Hears My Prayers

PRAISE GOD BECAUSE HE HEARS

*The eyes of the LORD are on the righteous
and his ears are attentive to their cry.*

PSALM 34:15

Dear Father, you are the Sovereign God, Creator and King over all of heaven and earth. Yet in your majestic greatness, you desire to hear the heart's cry of the ones you created. Your ears are attentive and alert to the prayers of your children. With words of praise I thank you for being ready and open to me when I seek you with a pure heart. I rejoice, Lord, that you delight to hear my prayers.

CONTINUED PRAISE:

God promises to answer your prayers (JEREMIAH 33:3; PSALM 17:6).
Your prayers are so valuable that God promises to save them (REVELATION 5:8).
God desires fellowship with you (REVELATION 3:20).
God teaches you to pray without ceasing (LUKE 18:1).

CONFESSION

"If my people, who are called by my name,
will humble themselves and pray and seek my face
and turn from their wicked ways, then will I hear from heaven
and will forgive their sin and will heal their land.
Now my eyes will be open and my ears attentive
to the prayers offered in this place," says the LORD.

2 CHRONICLES 7:14–15

Dear Lord, I confess to you those times I deliberately disobey, allowing my pride to surface and dictate my actions. Afterward I feel guilty and ashamed and wonder how you could forgive me again. Because of how I feel, I often doubt that if I seek your face and confess my sin, you will hear and immediately forgive me. Forgive me for trusting my feelings and doubting your promises to hear and heal.

REFLECTION: What keeps you from humbling yourself? Do you think there is something preventing God from hearing your prayers? Make some quiet time just for yourself, search your heart and see if there is something troubling you, something you need to confess. Remember, God who is faithful, always hears our prayers even when we don't think he does.

Thanksgiving

How gracious God will be when you cry for help!
As soon as he hears, he will answer you.

ISAIAH 30:19

Gracious Father, I give you great thanks
for being my Father who hears my prayers. I am blessed.
I feel so loved knowing that every concern I have is a concern to you.
Your promise assures me that you hear my prayers
and are working behind the scenes.
It is wonderful knowing you love to hear my voice.
I rejoice.

Continued Thanks

Be still and give joyous thanks for this truth:
In my distress I called to the LORD;
I cried to my God for help.
From his temple he heard my voice;
my cry came before him, into his ears.

PSALM 18:6

INTERCESSION

This is the confidence we have in approaching God:
that if we ask anything according to his will, he hears us.
And if we know that he hears us—whatever we ask—
we know that we have what we asked of him.

1 JOHN 5:14–15

Dear Father, I ask that you place in my child's heart a strong belief in your promise that as your child, he can approach you with confidence. May he know that anything he asks according to your will, you hear and will provide whatever he asks of you. Increase his faith. I ask that your words dwell richly in my child so he will ask according to your will. In Jesus' name, Amen.

CONTINUED INTERCESSION

Pray that your child knows God hears his prayer (MARK 11:23–24).
Pray for your child to gain a vision of the power of prayer (JAMES 5:16).
Pray he will learn to pray using the Scriptures (ISAIAH 55:11).
Pray your child will not be anxious about anything, but instead will pray
(PHILIPPIANS 4:6).

GOD'S PROMISE FOR YOUR CHILD

When my child cries out, and the LORD hears him;
he delivers him from all his troubles.

PSALM 34:17, AUTHOR'S PARAPHRASE

INTERSTATE INTERCESSION

"Honey, it's Toby! Can you get on the other phone?" My husband nodded and picked up the receiver in the study. After a rushed greeting, our son who was attending college out of state, launched into the purpose for the call. I could hear the panic in Toby's voice as he told us he had misplaced several checks from work. They'd simply disappeared!

Losing and misplacing things was not so disastrous when living at home. But Chicago was not home, and Mom was not there to help sort through bedroom piles and items tossed in the "circular file." As a typical mom who wants to fix things, I felt helpless. As a praying mom, however, I felt hopeful!

And pray we did, over the phone line. You could call it "interstate intercession." Toby prayed silently. I prayed that God's wisdom would extend to Toby and give him clear thinking and quick recall. His dad asked for the safe-keeping and quick recovery of the checks. When we said goodbye, I could detect a slight sigh of relief from Toby's end of the phone. Off the phone his father and I prayed that Toby would learn from this experience regardless of the outcome. We asked the Lord to reveal his faithfulness to Toby in ways that would expand his faith and confidence in answered prayer.

Less than an hour passed before the phone rang again. This time Toby's words were stumbling over each other as he shared the wonderful news. "Mom, I found them! Can you believe it? Thank you for praying with me!" We rejoiced together at God's quick response. Toby's following comment reflected a transparency he seldom risked, "Mom, when I come home for spring break, could we spend some time talking about prayer?" These simple words were music to a praying mom's heart.

Mom, I Need to Trust God's Plan for Me

PRAISE GOD BECAUSE HE IS SOVEREIGN

"For my thoughts are not your thoughts,
neither are your ways my ways," declares the LORD.
"As the heavens are higher than the earth, so are my ways higher than
your ways and my thoughts than your thoughts."

ISAIAH 55:8–9

Dear Father, I lift praises to you the Sovereign Lord, the God above all gods. You made the heavens and the earth by your great power. Nothing is too difficult for you. As Ruler over all, you reign from your holy throne with wisdom, power, and unfailing love. I bless your name that your kingdom is everlasting. I worship you, O mighty King. There is none like you.

CONTINUED PRAISE

God is the creator and owner of everything
(GENESIS 1:1; REVELATION 4:11; 1 CHRONICLES 29:11).
God has ultimate authority (1 TIMOTHY 6:15).
God is able to do what he wills (PSALM 135:6; EPHESIANS 3:20).

CONFESSION

God who began a good work in you
will carry it on to completion until the day of Christ Jesus.
PHILIPPIANS 1:6

Heavenly Father,
I feel like everything is falling apart in my life.
I am overwhelmed in my circumstances and at times wonder
where you are. Forgive me for doubting that you are
doing good work in my child's life.
Help me to remember this especially when I see him
making choices that are hurting him.
Forgive me for being fretful and fearful instead of trusting.
My Father, in the midst of unknowns I do not want to be afraid,
but want to trust in your sovereign,
loving plan for my child's life.

REFLECTION: Ask God to heal your fearful heart. Remember, only Jesus Christ can cleanse you and bring the peace you long for. Relinquish your anxieties to God, for he cares for you.

Thanksgiving

I know that you can do all things, Lord;
no plan of yours can be thwarted.

JOB 42:2

Father, what an incredible display of your sovereignty—
your plans are not thwarted.
I rejoice that no angel, person, or circumstance
can stop your plan for my life or for my children.
Nothing occurs in our lives without your divine permission,
and for that I am thankful.
Thank you for allowing the difficulties in our lives
to make us more like Jesus.

Continued Thanks

Thank God for the difference it makes in your life when you trust in his sovereign plan. Rejoice that there is nothing touching you or your children outside the will of God.

Intercession

"For I know the plans I have for you," declares the LORD, "plans to prosper you and not to harm you, plans to give you hope and a future."

JEREMIAH 29:11

Loving God, I pray that my child might know the plans you have for him; plans to prosper him and not to harm him, plans to give him a hope and a future. May this truth be his confidence and sweet peace throughout his life journey. I ask that he will feel loved and special knowing you scheduled each day of his life before he began to breathe. O Lord, I ask that he will live daily in your sovereign love, trusting you in all his ways without hesitation. In Jesus' name, Amen.

Continued Intercession

Pray for your child to know that God will work all things together for the good of those who love him. (ROMANS 8:28).

Pray that he will trust in the name of the Lord, not in people or things (PSALM 118:9; PSALM 20:7).

Ask God to reveal to your child that he cares about the smallest details of his life (MATTHEW 10:29–31).

Pray that he worships the sovereign God (PSALM 71:16).

God's Promise for Your Child

Commit to the LORD whatever you do, and your plans will succeed.

PROVERBS 16:3

BLUE SHOES

Our church was launching the first presentation of a well-respected abstinence program. As a mom of a 14-year-old son, I could hardly wait. But suddenly I remembered a baseball game was scheduled for the same time. As team pitcher, my son Josh needed to be at the game. As a Christian adolescent living in a "whatever feels good" culture, Josh needed to hear biblical principles concerning sexual purity, but he was also a team player and felt his responsibility was with the team.

As I prayed that morning, I was sure I knew just how God could fix this little schedule wrinkle. Rain. That would work. But every time I checked the sky, the day grew more radiant and cloudless. My exuberant faith shifted to disappointment as game time drew near. Apparently, God had not understood the importance of my request.

Josh descended the stairs at 5:00 p.m. in full uniform and glove in hand, ready for his game, but before we reached the door, the phone rang. "Mrs. Hanes, Coach Ballard here. The game's been cancelled."

Confused, I checked the sky one last time.

"Strangest thing. They had to cancel all the games tonight. It seems there was something sprayed on the fields, and it's turning everyone's shoes blue!"

I danced around the kitchen while my son gave me a look that said, "She's nuts!" As I explained about the field and the shoes turning blue, Josh's face broke into a grin.

We went to church that night, and the program was a "grand-slam." I think he was as impressed and as surprised as I was with God's creative answer to the schedule conflict. Since then he has often asked me to pray for him.

Thanks to God's sovereign hand and blue-tinted shoes, my son's faith, and my own, is stronger.

Mom, I Need Encouragement Today

PRAISE GOD BECAUSE HE IS FAITHFUL

O LORD God Almighty, who is like you?
You are mighty, O LORD, and your faithfulness surrounds you.

PSALM 89:8

O Lord, great is your faithfulness. It defines your very character. You are the faithful God whose ways are perfect and whose promises are sure. No matter what challenges or difficulties I have encountered, you have always been there to encourage me and give me hope. You are changeless, and your mercies and compassions never fail. You are faithful to provide all that I need and show me the path I should travel. With a joyful heart I proclaim that you are the same yesterday, today, and forever, my faithful God.

CONTINUED PRAISE

God's faithfulness continues throughout all generations (PSALM 100:5).
Praise God for his infinite and loving faithfulness (PSALM 57:10; 89:14).
God is faithful in all that he does (ISAIAH 41:13).

CONFESSION

God is faithful; he will not let you be tempted
beyond what you can bear.
But when you are tempted, he will also provide a way out
so that you can stand up under it.

1 CORINTHIANS 10:13

Dear Lord, please help me to be an encourager
to each member of my family.
Lately I find myself caught up in unrealistic expectations
that cause me to be critical and condemning.
I know my behavior and comments can crush the spirit of my children,
causing distance between us. I am so sorry.
Please help me to be their greatest cheerleader.
I truly want to be the wind beneath their wings

REFLECTION: In quietness and trust is your confidence. Ask the Holy Spirit to search your heart and open it to receiving God's love and encouragement. Experience the truth of God's faithful promise that he will forgive you so you can be supportive of your child.

Thanksgiving

This I call to mind and therefore I have hope:
Because of the LORD's great love we are not consumed,
for his compassions never fail.
They are new every morning; great is your faithfulness.

LAMENTATIONS 3:21–23

Father, I am filled with loving gratitude
for the promise that your mercies are new every morning.
No matter where life takes me,
your mercies are more than adequate to meet each need;
you give strength when I am weak, wisdom when I am confused,
and encouragement when I am fearful.
I rest, knowing your loving faithfulness surrounds my children and me.

Continued Thanks

Thank God for the family and friends he has brought into your life to encourage you. Give thanks for the people you have been able to encourage with your support.

Intercession

You are a shield around me, O LORD;
you bestow glory on me and lift up my head.

PSALM 3:3

Dear Father, I ask you to be a shield around my child, be his glory and the lifter of his head. Please come alongside of him through the power of your Holy Spirit and change his "I cannot" to "I can." May he find hope and encouragement through your Word. May he know that every day is full of opportunity and hope because of his faithful God. If his head is downcast because of sins, I pray that he will humble himself and ask for forgiveness. I ask that he will feel your faithful touch lifting his head once again. In Jesus' name, Amen.

Continued Intercession

Pray he will know God's faithful provision for all his needs
(PHILIPPIANS 4:19).
Pray he will believe all God's promises (NUMBERS 23:19; HEBREWS 10:23).
Pray he experiences God's faithfulness even when his faith is shaken
(ROMANS 3:3–4).

God's Promise for Your Child

No matter how many promises God has made, they are "Yes" in Christ.
And so through him the "Amen" is spoken by us to the glory of God.

2 CORINTHIANS 1:20

Across the Ocean

Have you ever had an answer to prayer travel across the ocean and land in your mailbox? My traveling answer arrived during a season when I was yearning to see tangible signs of spiritual growth in my children. Although my prayers were constant, any observable evidence was absent. I must admit, I had more than one "pity-party" over my teen's lack of spiritual appetite.

One day I dragged myself down the long driveway to retrieve the day's mail. A curious letter with a foreign stamp and postmark caught my eye. I opened it quickly and was greeted by the welcoming words of a young man I had met on a mission trip. I recognized the inquisitive, warm face on the enclosed photograph and smiled at the hints of young manhood emerging. This photo would replace the one I had posted in my prayer journal as a prompt to intercede for this young man whom I had spiritually adopted.

His letter was brief and poignant, his words penetrating to the core of my heart. "I want to thank you for praying for me and leading me to Jesus. I am living for Christ and serving Him as a street evangelist," he wrote.

I stood in the driveway, sobbing over this letter. The truth is, God's perfect timing and tender encouragement overwhelmed me as he revealed his faithfulness in answer to my prayer for a child halfway around the world. As I placed the letter on the top of the stack, I felt my doubt lifting. The Lord had proven himself faithful to my foreign friend—and to me. He sent word from a distant land to remind me that the best thing I can do for my own children is pray… and wait.

Mom, I Want to Grow Spiritually Mature

PRAISE GOD BECAUSE HE IS RIGHTEOUS

*You ... did not come to know Christ that way. Surely you heard of him
and were taught in him in accordance with the truth that is in Jesus.
You were taught, with regard to your former way of life ...
to be made new in the attitude of your minds; and to put on the new self,
created to be like God in true righteousness and holiness.*

EPHESIANS 4:20–24

*My Righteous God, you and you alone are worthy to receive this song of
praise —"Glory to the Righteous One"(Isaiah 24:16). You are the ultimate
standard for all that is right, pure, and moral. Everything you do is honor-
able, ethical, and virtuous. My soul rejoices that you are a righteous judge
who rules and reigns with unfailing love, grace, and compassion. I cherish
the truth that your righteousness endures forever.*

CONTINUED PRAISE

Praise God, all his words and actions are righteous (PSALM 19:9; JOEL 2:23).
God's righteousness is accompanied with grace and compassion (PSALM 116:5).
Through faith in Christ, man is righteous
(PHILIPPIANS 3:8–9; 2 CORINTHIANS 5:21).

Confession

Pursue righteousness, godliness, faith, love,
endurance and gentleness. Fight the good fight of the faith.
Take hold of the eternal life to which you were called when
you made your good confession in the presence of many witnesses.

1 Timothy 6:11–12

Dear Forgiving Father, I confess I get caught up in the pursuit of things that do not reflect your righteousness. I find myself in bondage to self-indulgence and bad habits. Please forgive me for allowing my mind to go places where you would not travel. I desire to be a righteous and gentle person. Fill me with your Holy Spirit and empower me to be a godly woman. May all that I do bring you glory.

REFLECTION: Take some personal time for reflection. Can you identify any bad habits or self-indulgences standing in the way of you becoming a righteous person? Write your thoughts on a piece of paper—truly repent—and experience God's amazing grace and forgiveness. Tear up the paper and throw it away. You are forgiven, and free to pursue righteousness.

Thanksgiving

Just as you received Christ Jesus as Lord,
continue to live in him, rooted and built up in him,
strengthened in the faith as you were taught,
and overflowing with thankfulness.

COLOSSIANS 2:6–7

Dear Righteous Father, I am overflowing with thankfulness. The moment I trusted in Christ as my Savior, you no longer saw my sins. I want to become righteous in your eyes. Jesus wiped out all my sin at the cross. What an exchange—my sin for Jesus' righteousness. There is no greater gift than that, and yet you give me more through your promises. You watch over all my ways and lead me in paths of righteousness for your name's sake (Psalm 23:3), and you bless me and surround me with favor (Psalm 5:12). I am unable to find the words that express my grateful heart for this great and awesome truth—so I simply, but sincerely, say, thank you.

REFLECTION: Mediate on what it means that Christ's righteousness became yours when you accepted Jesus into your heart. Thank him for every wonderful detail and circumstance of your salvation. Let the above promises sink deep into your heart.

INTERCESSION

*May he strengthen your hearts so that you will be
blameless and holy in the presence of our God and Father
when our Lord Jesus comes with all his holy ones.*

1 THESSALONIANS 3:13

*My Lord, I pray that you will strengthen my child's heart so he will be
blameless and holy in the presence of our God and Father when the Lord
Jesus comes with all his holy ones. Fill him with your Holy Spirit so he
might hunger and thirst for righteousness, wanting to do things pleasing to
you and that bring you glory. May his walk be strengthened through study
of your Word. May he be found diligent in prayer, including you in every
part of his life. I pray that growing in faith will be my child's main priority.
In Jesus' powerful name, Amen.*

CONTINUED INTERCESSION

Pray your child will seek the Lord first (MATTHEW 6:33).
Pray for your child to grow in the grace and knowledge of Jesus (2 PETER 3:18).
Ask God to lead your child into his light (EPHESIANS 5:8–10).
Pray he will stay true to his faith and not be deceived (COLOSSIANS 2:8).

GOD'S PROMISE TO YOUR CHILD

God will guide my child in the paths of righteousness for his name's sake.

PSALM 23:3, AUTHOR'S PARAPHRASE

WE GIVE OUR VERY BEST

In touch with You, dear Father, We come to You in prayer;
Our little lambs, our children, We lift up to Your care—
So much that we can give them, Yet so few things that last;
Committed, Lord, to pray for them. We give our very best.
CONNIE KENNEMER. ©1987 MITI

My son Todd was in kindergarten when I wrote the Moms In Touch (MITI) theme song. The visual image of a tender, helpless little lamb illustrated the very heart of this prayer ministry that placed the prayer needs of our children at the focal point of our weekly gatherings.

As I prepared music for a recent MITI retreat, these lyrics gripped me like never before. Mental movie clips flashed by as I reviewed my 16-year commitment to pray for my son. What a thrilling adventure it has been and continues to be. My tender lamb is no longer helpless, no longer little. He is now a confident young man with a burning passion for God. The life seasons have changed. Distant are the days when I held his hand as we crossed busy streets. He is grown now and capable of protecting me when we walk. But he can never stretch and grow past his need for my prayers. His needs are not seasonal, just like a mighty oak tree always requires the sun and water to thrive.

My son now lives in the Mission District of San Francisco among the poor and disenfranchised. His work takes him around the streets of Golden Gate Park with the homeless, lost, and wounded sheep on Haight Street. He ministers to them as a young adult among his peers.

A decade and a half ago I began to pray faithfully for my son. The practice continues today. I often catch my breath as I think of him on the San Francisco streets—my grown up lamb living among lost sheep, guiding them to the Good Shepherd.

A lifetime of faithful prayer is the very best gift we can give.

Mom, I Need Strength to Choose Right from Wrong

PRAISE GOD BECAUSE HE IS MY STRENGTH

*It is God who arms me with strength
and makes my way perfect.*

2 SAMUEL 22:23

I love you, O Lord, my strength. I marvel at your strength that I see in your creation, in your deliverance, in your Spirit within me, and your Word that enables me to do right. I praise you for the promise of your strength to those who ask for it. I rejoice that your strength is always available and replaces my weariness with endurance and hope. I declare with joy that you alone have the power to transform my heart. Your Almighty power cannot be diminished. I will praise your glorious power forever.

CONTINUED PRAISE

God's strength is our joy (NEHEMIAH 8:10).
Through God's strength we are victorious (HEBREWS 11:32–34).
God's strength is abundant (EPHESIANS 1:18).
God's strength enables us to do all things (PHILIPPIANS 4:13).

CONFESSION

I am the vine; you are the branches.
If a man remains in me and I in him, he will bear much fruit;
apart from me you can do nothing," says the Lord.

JOHN 15:5

Dear Lord, I admit that I am trying to handle things myself. I have been looking to my own resources and that of others instead of looking to you, leaving me tired, weak, and defeated. Forgive me for relying on myself. Help me to remain in you and rely in your strength to do right.

REFLECTION: Take a few moments to reflect on all of the decisions you make each day and all of the things you do. Are you relying on your own strength instead of God's strength? What areas in your life do you need to turn over to God? The Lord will give you the strength do to what is right if you listen to what he is telling you to do.

Thanksgiving

Whom have I in heaven but you?
And earth has nothing I desire besides you.
My flesh and my heart may fail,
but God is the strength of my heart
and my portion forever.

Psalm 73:25–26

Dear Mighty Father, thank you for your strength that is perfect when I am weak. Thank you for sending Jesus to save me from the battle of good and evil within me. Your Word gives me the wisdom to know right from wrong. I know it is your power that helps me to keep praying when the answers haven't come yet. It is your strength that transforms my heart and helps me to do your perfect will. I rejoice that you are the strength of my life!

Continued Thanks

Can you recall a specific example of when the Lord's strength enabled you to overcome a difficult time in your life? Have you thanked him? In what other ways have you felt his power working through you?

Intercession

Be strong in the Lord and in his mighty power. Put on the full armor of God, so that when the day of evil comes, you may be able to stand your ground, and after you have done everything, to stand. Stand firm then, with the belt of truth buckled around your waist, with the breastplate of righteousness in place, and with your feet fitted with the readiness that comes from the gospel of peace.

EPHESIANS 6:10, 13–15

O Lord my Strength, I pray for my child to be strong in you and in your mighty power. I pray that she will put on the full armor of God and is able to stand her ground. I pray she will hunger to know your Word and grow in spiritual wisdom and strength. May she stand firm with the belt of truth by walking in integrity, and rely on you to help her overcome the temptations in her life. May she wear the breastplate of righteousness by having a pure heart. With your help may she live a righteous lifestyle, understanding she can only do good through your strength. In Jesus' name, Amen.

Continued Intercession

Pray that your child is strengthened according to God's word (PSALM 119:28). Ask God to help your child to listen for his voice to guide her (ISAIAH 30:21). Pray that she may be strengthened by the Holy Spirit's power (EPHESIANS 3:16).

God's Promise for Your Child

Your child can do everything through Christ who gives him strength.

PHILIPPIANS 4:13, AUTHOR'S PARAPHRASE

LIFE CHOICES

When my 18-year old daughter Jess tearfully announced she was pregnant, I was shocked beyond belief. Jess had been on the receiving end of my consistent prayer since her birth. Heartbroken, I grieved the loss of her purity and dreaded the negative reaction of my husband. And in those turbulent moments I gave her advice that still stuns me. Always pro-life, I surprisingly yielded to the pressure of the moment and counseled her to make an appointment to have an abortion. I am horrified by the memory and what would have happened had she listened.

The following Friday I was gathered in prayer with my prayer partners. We prayed and cried together. I repented of the misdirected counsel I had given my daughter in a moment of emotional turmoil. They responded with the compassion and grace of Christ.

As I look back, I recognize the footprints of the enemy. He had been lurking behind my twisted perception of how my husband would handle the news. Instead, Jess was fully supported by her father who promised her we would walk through this as a family. Jess pursued open adoption and within months gave birth to sweet Kelly. Kelly soon left her mother's arms to take up residence in the waiting arms of a wonderful Christian couple.

This crisis became a life-defining event for my daughter. Jess currently speaks to teens and parents about the incredible blessings for those who consider or choose open adoption rather than abortion. I marvel at her courage. Her strength is a sharp contrast to the fear and panic that drove me.

The two of us love and serve a God who redeems—buys back— bad choices. For us, he turned them into a life choice—named Kelly.

Mom, I Need a Teachable Spirit

PRAISE GOD BECAUSE HE IS MY TEACHER

This is what the LORD says—I am your Redeemer, the Holy One of Israel:
"I am the LORD your God, who teaches you what is best for you,
who directs you in the way you should go."

ISAIAH 48:17

Dear Lord, you are the Supreme Teacher. There is no one who can give you counsel, for you are the source of all wisdom and knowledge. My tongue sings of your words, for all your "precepts are right, giving joy to my heart" (Psalm 19:8). What joy to know that your instructions are always for my good and that you are my personal teacher. I glory in your guidance that is uniquely designed for me. There is no Teacher like you.

CONTINUED PRAISE

God is the great teacher (ISAIAH 2:2–3).
God is our personal teacher (PSALM 71:17).
There is no one more knowledgeable than God (ISAIAH 40:10–14).

CONFESSION

Love the LORD your God with all your heart
and with all your soul and with all your strength.
These commandments that I give you today are to be upon
your hearts. Impress them on your children. Talk about them
when you sit at home and when you walk along the road,
when you lie down and when you get up. Do what is right and
good in the LORD's sight, so that it may go well with you.

DEUTERONOMY 6:5–7, 18

Dear Lord, I admit that I have not always been willing to learn. I have often ignored your guidance and have missed opportunities to teach my children your life-changing commands. Please forgive me. Please help me to listen to you and be open to receiving the lessons only you can teach. Help me to be a better student of your word. Send me your wisdom so I may teach my children without hesitation.

REFLECTION: Do you have a teachable spirit? In what areas of your life are you resisting the Lord's lessons and corrections? Go forward with new determination. God hears the desires of your heart and will help you.

Thanksgiving

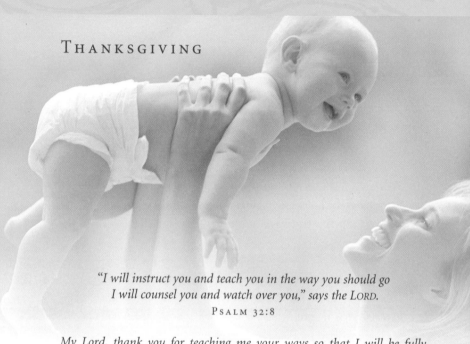

*"I will instruct you and teach you in the way you should go
I will counsel you and watch over you," says the LORD.*
PSALM 32:8

My Lord, thank you for teaching me your ways so that I will be fully instructed to follow in obedience. Your patience as a teacher is always personal, gracious, and kind. In your wisdom, you know the ways I learn best. I rejoice that you never give up on me, are always watching over me, and give me timely counsel for every decision. Thank you for the loving way you instruct me. I trust you to help me teach my children.

CONTINUED THANKS

Can you remember something that God has had to teach you time and again until you finally got it? Thank him for being such a patient, loving teacher.

INTERCESSION

Teach me to do your will, for you are my God;
may your good Spirit lead me on level ground.

PSALM 143:10

Father, I pray you will teach my child your way, because you are her God.
May she willingly let the Holy Spirit lead and guide her on level ground.
May your words always ring true in her mind. I ask you to fill her with
your Holy Spirit and guide her into all truth. May she desire to bring you
honor and glory throughout her life. I ask that she will be attentive to the
godly counsel of others and open to loving rebuke. Help her also to be
open in receiving your great knowledge. Please give me wisdom and
assistance in pointing her to the truth. In Jesus' name, Amen.

CONTINUED INTERCESSION

Pray your child will be open to receiving God's lessons (PSALM 86:11).
Pray that your child will always seek truth (PROVERBS 18:15; JOHN 14:6).
Ask God to help her learn from godly rebuke (PROVERBS 1:23, 29–31, 33).
Pray that she obeys God's instruction (PROVERBS 4:20–23).

GOD'S PROMISE FOR YOUR CHILD:

Your children will be taught by the LORD, and great will be their peace.

ISAIAH 54:13 AUTHOR'S PARAPHRASE

A Testimony in Progress

At 19, my daughter Heather is a "reluctant" Christian. On Valentine's Day when she was three years old, she announced that she had asked Jesus into her heart. For the rest of her childhood she grew in grace. I called her my little evangelist. God had given her a spirit of compassion and mercy and boldness. She was always sharing the gospel with friends and strangers.

Then at about age 14, Heather said she "got gypped out of a testimony." She said the speakers at youth camp all had great stories about living in sin and how Jesus rescued them. She said she wanted a great story to tell, too.

"What am I going to say, 'I've been to church every Sunday since I was two weeks old?' What kind of a testimony is that?" she asked.

I told her that was a good testimony, but she didn't think so. This was the beginning of her walking away from fellowship with God.

As a mother, my heart aches for her to return. My prayer has been and continues to be, "Lord, soften her heart; give her a teachable spirit. Don't let her forget the truth."

And he has answered that prayer. More often than not when her wandering has led her into dark places, she eventually comes home and seeks me out to talk. We've had good discussions, even if she doesn't always take my advice or God's.

Yet as hard as she runs or tries to hide from the Lord, Heather knows she belongs to him. Frankly, that annoys her at this stage in her life.

Still … she always comes back to the truth. She always returns to the things she learned and loved as a child. Even if just for a brief moment, she always comes back to the Lord.

I'm praying for the day she stays. What a testimony she'll have then.

Mom, I'm Struggling with My School Work

PRAISE GOD BECAUSE HE IS MY HELPER

My help comes from the LORD,
the Maker of heaven and earth.

PSALM 121:2

Dear Lord, I praise you that you are with me to help me in all my ways. What a blessing to know that I can count on you to help me in any given situation and at any moment, especially when I am feeling vulnerable, weak, overwhelmed, or fearful. When I cry out to you in my distress, no matter how big or small the need, I know you hear me. I praise you, my Eternal God. It brings great comfort and confidence to my heart. I love you, O Lord, my helper.

CONTINUED PRAISE

God promises to help (ISAIAH 41:14).
God has the power to help (2 CHRONICLES 25:8).
God hears your cry for help and answers (PSALM 18:6).
God's help is sure (PSALM 54:4).

CONFESSION

Let us then approach the throne of grace with confidence,
so that we may receive mercy and find grace to help us in our time of need.
HEBREWS 4:16

Dear Heavenly Father, I confess that I try to handle things on my own without
seeking your help. I do not want to admit to you or to others that I need help.
Forgive me for my pride. I'm sorry for not including you in my everyday life.

REFLECTION: Are you struggling with particular situations or people in
your life? Have you asked God for help and guidance? Tell the Lord of your
struggles, and he will hear your cry for help. Allow God to lighten your burden.

Thanksgiving

With your help I can advance against a troop;
with my God I can scale a wall.

2 Samuel 22:30

Dear caring Father, thank you for coming to my aid every time I seek your help and for always responding to me with loving-kindness. I rejoice that with your help I have the strength and resolve to tackle hard situations and am able to make progress. As a mom I need strength, patience, wisdom, and so much more. Thank you for truly being there to help when I ask you. What a relief it is to know that I do not have to handle everything myself. Because of your help, I sing in the shadow of your wings (Psalm 63:7).

Continued Thanks

Think carefully over this past week. What are some ways you have experienced God's help in raising your children? Can you recall other ways you have experienced God's help? Give thanks specifically for that help.

INTERCESSION

*I am the LORD, your God, who takes hold of your right hand
and says to you, Do not fear; I will help you.*

ISAIAH 41:13

Dear Loving Father, I pray that my child will experience you taking hold of his right hand and hearing your words: "Do not fear; I will help you." This will be reassuring to him as he struggles with his studies at school. Please give his teachers patience, compassion, and wisdom to know how to help him learn. I pray that he will not be too proud or embarrassed to ask his teacher for help. Give him quick understanding of his lessons, enlighten his mind and protect him from discouragement. Grant him peace and contentment when he knows that he has tried his best. In Jesus' name, Amen.

CONTINUED INTERCESSION

Pray your child will ask God for his wisdom (JEREMIAH 33:3).
Pray that your child will work with all his heart to please God
(COLOSSIANS 3:23).
Pray that his teachers will be encouraging (1 THESSALONIANS 5:14).

GOD'S PROMISE TO YOUR CHILD

*Your child can say with confidence, "The Lord is my helper;
I will not be afraid. What can man do to me?"*
HEBREWS 13:6, AUTHOR'S PARAPHRASE

CAN I QUIT—PLEASE?

My seventh grader Joshua had always been good in math; it just seemed to be easy for him. So it was no surprise when he was chosen to participate in an advanced math class. We allowed him to make the switch, pleased that his teacher had confidence in his readiness. But our excitement sagged when Joshua began coming home from math class upset and occasionally in tears.

Joshua's "dark nights of homework" were painful to watch. I could sense the struggle within him as he battled a lack of confidence and uncertainty with the new material. It was not long until he voiced the question that was bouncing around his tired little mind, "Can I quit? Please?"

His question prompted questions of my own. Do I meet with his teacher for her counsel or do I simply retreat to my prayer closet? I chose to do both. My Moms In Touch prayer team joined me in praying that God would help Joshua in his accelerated course. My heart was encouraged by our prayer times, but I still ached when I saw Joshua's continued pain and confusion during the homework hour.

Then my appointment with his instructor was cancelled. While this left me frustrated, it also reminded me that persevering in prayer was my best (and only) option. As I aligned myself with God's heart for Joshua, I began to see Joshua's attitude soften and the material grow easier for him to understand. I knew we'd turned an important corner.

Joshua was all smiles as he presented his report card with an "A-" in advanced math. "You know, Mom, I really think I'm getting used to this math teacher. And the assignments just don't bother me like they used to."

Joshua was desperate for help, and God came through. I learned that divine appointments in prayer are never postponed, and they don't need to be

Mom, I Want to Feel Confident

PRAISE GOD BECAUSE HE IS ABLE

*Ah, Sovereign LORD you have made the heavens and the earth
by your outstretched arm. Nothing is too hard for you.*

JEREMIAH 32:17

*Dear Father, You are ABLE. I am in awe of the truth that nothing
is too difficult for you. You are capable, skillful, competent, masterful,
and all sufficient. I marvel that you can do anything.
When I think about the heavens, the moon, all the stars, and how you
are able to hold everything together by your infinite power,
there is no doubt in my heart that you are able to meet all my needs
and enable me to do anything you ask. In Jesus' name, Amen.*

CONTINUED PRAISE

God is able to save you (HEBREWS 7:25).

God is able to restore our losses (JOEL 2:25).

Nothing will separate you from God's love (ROMANS 8:38–39).

God is able to do more than what we ask or imagine (EPHESIANS 3:20).

CONFESSION

He who trusts in himself is a fool,
but he who walks in wisdom is kept safe.

PROVERBS 28:26

Dear Father, there are many time when I feel inadequate. I often complain that I don't have the personal qualities necessary to do specific tasks. I procrastinate, despair, or give up. You are able to make all grace abound to me for everything that I need to be successful. Help me to replace fear of failure with confidence and rely on your sufficiency.

REFLECTION: Ask God to help you identify the times in your life when you didn't feel able to do what God asked because you were not confident in your abilities. Were you relying on your own strength and not God's? Give these situations to him. God is able to give you full confidence through his grace.

Thanksgiving

*I know whom I have believed, and am convinced that he is able
to guard what I have entrusted to him for that day.*

2 Timothy 1:12

*My dear Able God, I greatly rejoice in the comforting promise that you are
able to guard my children as I entrust them to you through prayer. It gives
me such confidence to know you are protecting them when they encounter
feelings of exclusion or insecurity. I am so grateful that each morning as
they go off to school you are going with them. I'm encouraged by the
thought that you keep them under surveillance, watching over their day.
What a relief to know that you are able to provide them with faith and
strength to withstand whatever their day brings. I am so grateful that I can
entrust my children to a God who is able to keep his promises.*

Continued Thanks

Give thanks by reflecting on the list below. Rest in the confidence that
God is able to:

Give you guidance when you have no idea what to do.

Provide for your child's needs in answer to your prayers.

Give courage in the face of fear.

INTERCESSION

God is able to make all grace abound to you, so that in all things at all times, having all that you need, you will abound in every good work.

2 CORINTHIANS 9:8

Dear Gracious Father, I ask that your grace will abound to my child so that in all things at all times, having all that she needs, she will abound in every good work. Lord, my child doubts her talents and abilities. She feels incapable and lacks confidence. I pray for your grace to be in her life so she will be able to excel in the abilities that you have given her. Protect her from the harm and damage of comparison to others. Oh Lord, help her recognize that you have uniquely created her with special gifts and talents. Help me as a mother to recognize her capabilities, and grant me your wisdom to know how to nurture and encourage her. In Jesus' name, Amen.

CONTINUED INTERCESSION

Pray for your child's continued self-confidence (2 TIMOTHY 1:6–7).
Ask God to assure your child that through Christ she can do all things
(PHILIPPIANS 4:13).
Pray your child gives careful attention to her unique gifts
(PROVERBS 22:29).
Pray for her confidence in God's plan for her (PSALM 118:8).

GOD'S PROMISE FOR YOUR CHILD

Commit to the LORD whatever you do, and your plans will succeed.

PROVERBS 16:3

SOLID GROUND

Erin's third grade year had a wobbly start. Her days were filled with cold shoulders, favoritism, and whispers that caused her to feel abandoned and emotionally drained. In addition, Erin had a teacher who did not support her. School was anything but safe for my eight-year-old.

I watched from the sidelines as Erin's self-confidence plummeted. She was convinced that no one liked her. I fervently prayed that the Lord would fill Erin with confidence, help her understand that she was his perfect design, and reassure her that he smiled every time he looked at this masterpiece named Erin.

There are seasons of prayer when we wait to see God's handiwork and others where God rushes in to show himself strong. How I praise him that in this case he answered quickly for my daughter. Later that very year we saw Erin relieved of the negative relationships and emotional distress. A new freedom followed that seemed to empower her.

I saw continued evidence of the power of prayer when she won three awards at school and received the accolades of her classmates. As peers "high-fived" her and verbally acknowledged her gifts and talents, I saw this self-conscious little girl blossom before my very eyes. Only God could convince Erin that she is a jewel, and I'm confident he had something to do with the peer-approval as well.

Three years later, when Erin was in middle school, our family reconnected with friends we hadn't seen for some time. I chuckle now as I recall my girlfriend's observation, "Your daughter is SO confident. You must be pleased." Answered prayer is a delightful gift of our capable God. He took a tentative eight-year-old and transformed her into a confident child who likes the way God made her.

Life will probably have more bumps, but for now Erin is stepping lively. She knows where to plant her feet and has learned to trust in herself and God.

Mom, I Need to Use My Time Wisely

PRAISE GOD BECAUSE HE IS WISE

Praise be to the name of God for ever and ever;
wisdom and power are his."

DANIEL 2:20

Dear Lord, what security I have in knowing that you are the God of all wisdom. I praise your power and unlimited ability to discern and judge what is true and right. Your creation is a wonderful revelation of your magnificent wisdom. I marvel at the depth of your wisdom and knowledge. I glory in you, my wise God. Praise the Lord!

CONTINUED PRAISE

God is eternal (GENESIS 21:3; DANIEL 4:34).

God is timeless (PSALM 90:2; 2 PETER 3:8).

In his wisdom, God determines the steps of our days (PROVERBS 16:9).

God's wisdom is beyond measure (ROMANS 11:33).

CONFESSION

Dear God, I find myself wasting precious time
on things that really don't matter.
It is so easy for me to take the path of lease resistance
and miss opportunities for the little things that can mean so much.
Sometimes my life seems so overwhelming
that I find it difficult to keep moving.
Forgive me for not using my time wisely.
Help met to take seriously the brevity of life,
and that it is what I do for you that really counts.
I want to honor you with my time and service to others.

REFLECTION: How are you using your time? Wisely? Do you frequently hear yourself saying "no" to requests for your time to help others because you are too busy? Search your heart and think about what is important to God. There is a time and a place for everything. With God's wisdom and guidance, you will find the answers.

THANKSGIVING

This is the day the LORD has made; let us rejoice and be glad in it.

PSALM 118:24

Dear all wise God. I thank you for each new day. Your ways are perfect; you cannot make a mistake. In your infinite wisdom you have ordained each day of my life. I anticipate my tomorrows with wonder. Thank you for each new day filled with challenges, adventures, discoveries, and situations that bring me closer to you. I will rejoice and be glad in it!

MEMORIZE THIS VERSE, GIVING THANKS FOR ITS TRUTHS:

Your eyes saw my unformed body.
All the days ordained for me were written in your book
before one of them came to be.

How precious to me are your thoughts, O God!
How vast is the sum of them!

PSALM 139:16–17

INTERCESSION

Teach us to number our days aright,
that we may gain a heart of wisdom.

PSALM 90:12

Dear Lord, I ask that you will teach my child to number his days rightly so he may gain a heart of wisdom. I pray that above all things he will seek you first, for the fear of the Lord is the beginning of wisdom. The wise man builds his life on the truths of your word; may this be true of my child. Help him to be self-disciplined and diligent with a keen sense of responsibility for his time. My Father, please help my child use the wisdom you give him to bring honor and glory to you. In Jesus' name, Amen.

CONTINUED INTERCESSION

Pray that your child will seek the Lord's face always (1 CHRONICLES 16:11).
Pray that he becomes wise through the word (PSALM 19:7–8; MATTHEW 7:24).
Pray your child will be filled with the knowledge of God's will

(COLOSSIANS 1:9).

Ask God to help your child set his mind on eternal things

(COLOSSIANS 3:1–2; 1 CORINTHIANS 13:12).

GOD'S PROMISE FOR YOUR CHILD

If any of you lacks wisdom, he should ask God,
who gives generously to all without finding fault, and it will be given to him.

JAMES 1:5

THE TREEHOUSE

When my son Adam was fourteen, he was obsessed with the silver screen. His love for movies monopolized every waking moment of his life outside of eating, sleeping, and homework (involuntary, but required). There was no question that when Adam and his friends got together what the chosen activity would be.

Every free moment, Adam plugged a cassette into the VCR or went channel surfing. My concern heightened as Adam's interest in the opposite sex soared (puberty does that, you know). The TV screen paints a jaded picture of what is normal and acceptable in male/female relationships.

As my concern grew, so did my desire to pray for Adam. I realized I couldn't force him to do the internal work that would break this addiction to the screen. So I left it with the Lord.

I was stunned when Adam came to me a few weeks later asking if he could tear down his brother's old treehouse to build a new one. He turned toward Larry, his best friend, as he continued his plea. "You know, Mom, we watch way too much TV and movies. This would give us something productive to do with our free time." Larry nodded in agreement. I blinked and shook my head, making sure this wasn't just a dream.

Adam rallied his friends and built a new treehouse. Two years have passed and this project has been successfully completed. This construction company of teens built a top-rate treehouse. It is three stories high, has windows and doors, is painted inside and out, and is furnished with bunk beds and assorted garage sale furniture. With this accomplishment behind them, Adam and his friends are trying their hand at landscaping. Will wonders never cease?

Old habits may be hard to break, but when God answers prayer, those habits are dead and buried. Adam and his friends still watch an occasional movie— they wired the treehouse for electricity—but for the most part, the silver screen monster has been tamed.

Mom, I Need to Grow Healthy and Strong

PRAISE GOD BECAUSE JESUS IS THE BREAD OF LIFE

Jesus declared, "I am the bread of life.
He who comes to me will never go hungry,
and he who believes in me will never be thirsty."

JOHN 6:35

Heavenly Father, I praise you for your son Jesus who satisfies my soul. Without bread the human body cannot be sustained; without food we would starve and perish. What bread is to the body, Christ is to the soul. I marvel at your unlimited supply of resources that nourish me and help me grow. Your words feed my soul and give me hope and guidance for living an abundant life here on earth. I praise you, Jesus, that you are my daily bread, satisfying the deepest hunger of my heart. I love you.

CONTINUED PRAISE

God is all we need (PSALM 23:1).

We live on the Word of God (MATTHEW 4:4).

God's words revive our souls (PSALM 19:7–11).

Obedience to God's words prolongs life (PROVERBS 3:1–4).

CONFESSION

Praise the LORD, O my soul, and forget not all his benefits—
who forgives all your sins and heals all your diseases,
who redeems your life from the pit and crowns you with love
and compassion, who satisfies your desires with good things
so that your youth is renewed like the eagle's.

PSALM 103:2–5

My Father, I am physically hurting.
My heart pounds with anxiety and my nerves are raw.
I have been carrying burdens that have taken the joy out of my life
and have left my body broken and depleted.
Forgive me for not trusting you with my cares.
I cast my burdens upon you. I can't carry them any more.
Come quickly my Lord.
Bring life back to my bones and peace to my soul.

REFLECTION: Are there sins in your life that are preventing you from being physically and spiritually healthy? Name them and give them to Jesus, he is strong. Feel the weight of the burden lifted from your shoulders to his. Feel his peace.

THANKSGIVING

Jesus said, "I tell you the truth, whoever hears my word
and believes him who sent me has eternal life and will not be condemned;
he has crossed over from death to life."

JOHN 5:24

Dear Jesus, I am forever grateful for the Bible.
I love the Scripture because it is the source of everything that I need
to grow in spiritual strength and wisdom.
Thank you for the times your words have brought me hope
and sustained me when I was crushed in my spirit and broken hearted.
With joy I acknowledge the ability of your words
to bring deep satisfaction to my heart that
material things of this world cannot.
Your words give life and bring health to my body.
I am profoundly grateful for the nourishment you provide
to my soul through the power of your word.

CONTINUED THANKS

Can you think of Scriptures that brought nourishment to your heart when
you were in need? If so, take time to write a thank you letter to Jesus.

Intercession

Trust in the LORD with all your heart and lean not on your own understanding;
in all your ways acknowledge him, and he will make your paths straight.
Do not be wise in your own eyes; fear the LORD and shun evil.
This will bring health to your body and nourishment to your bones.

Proverbs 3:5–8

Gracious Father, I pray that my child will trust in you with all her heart and lean not on her own understanding but acknowledge you in all her ways, and you will make her path straight. Thank you for the promise that this will bring health to her body. Father, there are so many harmful things that could damage her body. I pray against anything that might bring ill heath to her body and ultimately her soul. Protect her mind from temptation. May my child have a reverent fear of you, Lord, and desire only to please you. I pray that she will enjoy good health so she may serve you with great zeal. In Jesus' name, Amen.

Continued Intercession

Pray that she nourishes her soul through the reading of God's word
(Matthew 4:4).
Pray that drugs and alcohol will not lead her astray. (Proverbs 20:1).
Pray for your child to give God glory in whatever she eats or drinks
(1 Corinthians 10:31).

God's Promise for Your Child

Jesus said, "I have come that they may have life, and have it to the full."
John 10:10, author's paraphrase

Starving for Bread

My daughter, Alison, still remembers the exact moment she decided to stop eating. At age ten she was keenly aware that "thin is better than fat." Sadly, she learned that from me. I had always battled my weight and often involved her in conversations about losing ten more pounds and wishing I could be thin.

The next year or so was a battleground. Alison wouldn't eat and after a while, she couldn't eat. Her arms became like toothpicks, her skin turned gray, and she had dark circles under her eyes. I would take her to the market and offer to buy her anything if she would only eat it. She would either refuse or nibble on a piece of bread or a slice of turkey.

Whenever I tell this story to other moms they always ask, "What did you finally do to help her?" Honestly, I didn't do anything—except pray. I didn't know what else to do, but I knew that God did. I knew that Jesus, the Bread of Life, could feed my daughter when she couldn't—wouldn't—feed herself.

Ironically, what turned her around was a diet. I had joined a dieting Bible study group and learned to change my way of eating. Alison saw me losing weight, and in her child-logic she decided that if she followed my diet, she, too, would lose weight. Instead, as she started eating again she began feeling better: body, soul, and spirit. As she felt better, she ate more. Eventually, food lost its power over the two of us. Now fourteen years later, my daughter is healthy, whole, and the mother of my first grandchild.

I don't claim to have great faith. I do know that whenever I've fallen desperately on my knees before the Lord and begged him to be merciful to me and to my children, he has. Not only does he bestow his great mercy, he graciously prepares a table before us and invites us to feast with him and be nourished by him.

Mom, I Want to Feel Good About My Appearance

PRAISE GOD BECAUSE HE IS OUR CREATOR

Praise the LORD … Let them praise the name of the LORD, for he commanded and they were created.

PSALM 148:5

Creator God, you alone are the Maker of heaven and earth. You are the one who brought the universe and all life into existence. By your word you spoke all things into being out of nothing. The heavens and the earth declare your glory, blessed be your glorious name. I declare with Nehemiah, "You gave life to everything, and the multitude of heaven worship you" (Nehemiah 9:6). Your most magnificent act of creation was creating us after your own image. I praise you, Creator God, for everything you made is good!

CONTINUED PRAISE

God created the earth and mankind (ISAIAH 45:12).
God created all things by his word and the breath of his mouth
(PSALM 33:6, 9).
Everything God created is good (1 TIMOTHY 4:4).

79

CONFESSION

Jesus said, "Do not judge, and you will not be judged
Do not condemn, and you will not be condemned
Forgive, and you will be forgiven.

LUKE 6:37

Dear Lord, Forgive me for criticizing the way you made me. How many times have I wanted to change my appearance and not appreciated that you created me to be just the way I am? I have taken for granted the awesome works of your hands. I have also failed to give you glory by not living in a way that reflects your holiness and your beauty. Help me to become as beautiful on the inside as I want to be on the outside. Forgive me for those times I don't mirror your character.

REFLECTION: Do you spend more time trying to make your outward appearance beautiful than you spend letting God beautify your heart? Confess your vanity to God and ask him to forgive your preoccupation with your appearance. Ask Jesus to help you glorify him each day in all you do and say.

Thanksgiving

In the beginning God created the heavens and the earth.
GENESIS 1:1

Lord our Maker, I thank you for your awesome creation. I love the ocean that teems with sea life. It provides great enjoyment for the squealing toddler, dipping his toe for the first time in the waves. I delight in the beautiful varieties of flowers, each with its own unique fragrance. Thank you for the majestic mountains that rise with incomparable beauty and provide the perfect playground for fun and adventure. Thank you for the moon and the stars that cause our children to ask curious questions about your existence and offer a glorious night show. You formed my children in my womb and made them unique, too. Thank you Father for the wonder of our bodies. Your creation is too marvelous for words.

Continued Thanks

Read all of Psalm 139 whenever you feel down and tempted to question how you look. Read it again to remind yourself that you are fearfully and wonderfully made. Thank God for his attentive care over all he has made.

Intercession

*You created my inmost being, O Lord; you knit me together
in my mother's womb. I praise you because I am fearfully
and wonderfully made; your works are wonderful, I know that full well.*

Psalm 139:13–14

*My Father, you created my child's inmost being; you knit him together in my
womb. May he praise you because he is fearfully and wonderfully made; and
believe that your works are wonderful. I am very concerned because he thinks
he is not attractive and wants to alter his outward appearance. Oh Father,
please help him to know that you do not make mistakes; he was uniquely
designed by you for a specific purpose and beautiful to you. May this truth sink
deep into his soul. Enable him to change the things he can and be at peace with
the things he can't. Please give him victory in this area. I pray that he will have
a heart that reflects the beauty of Christ. In Jesus' name, Amen.*

Continued Intercession

Ask God to help your child understand he is God's masterpiece
(Ephesians 2:10).
Pray that he finds worth in being created for God's glory (Isaiah 43:1, 3–4,7).
Pray your child cares more about the condition of his heart
than outward appearances (1 Samuel 16:17).

God's Promise for Your Child

*The Lord does not look at the things man looks at. Man looks at the out-
ward appearance, but the Lord looks at the heart.*

1 Samuel 16:7

THE UGLY BOMB

The season of adolescence was full of anxious thoughts and stormy emotions for me. If that weren't enough, during my early teens I got hit with the "ugly bomb".

My fifteenth year was a series of "bad face days." First, it was the glasses, then the braces, and finally a crop of wild hair that looked like I had stuck my finger in a light socket. But acne was the bomb-blast that blew me away. I am not referring to an occasional pimple that I could hide or medicate. This was cystic acne that took over my face, my neck, my shoulders and my back.

Desperate for help, I attended a healing crusade, hoping that someone's prayer could break through God's silence. My mother agonized over my situation and prayed constantly, but the scars and pocks continued to mock me each time I saw my reflection in the mirror.

I know now that my acne-trauma was the subject of many weekly Moms In Touch prayers. It was there that Mom connected with Sondra whose son had a similar struggle with acne. He had recently started a powerful antibiotic that had made a radical difference. Sondra's answered prayer for her son fueled my mother's conviction that nothing was too big for her wonderful God. She couldn't wait to tell me. I started the treatment very soon and within six months the acne began to disappear. It was a miracle, and I knew it.

I am thirty years old now and a first-time father. Little Joshua's face is perfect and innocent. Now I am the grown-up, looking down the road at guiding my young son through his own adolescence. Try as I might, I won't be able to protect him from all that life throws his way. But I can give him the gifts my mother gave me: unwavering prayer and unstoppable faith. I will follow her example, praying and trusting the God of the Impossible. Count on it, Joshua.

Mom, I Need Physical Healing

PRAISE GOD BECAUSE HE IS THE GREAT PHYSICIAN

I am the LORD, who heals you.

EXODUS 15:26

My Great Physician, I praise you that you are the source of all healing,
healing all manner of diseases and sicknesses.
As the Lord who heals, you have shown yourself
to be compassionate, caring, and full of mercy.
How great is your love that you heal
and make whole with unlimited power.
I praise you that your healing touch is lovingly applied
and perfectly timed. Truly you are the Great Physician.

CONTINUED PRAISE

God is the author of healing (PSALM 103:2–3).
God's mercy and healing power come through Jesus (ACTS 10:37–38).
Heaven is the place of ultimate healing (REVELATION 21:4;
PHILIPPIANS 3:20–21).

CONFESSION

The LORD has not despised or disdained the suffering of the afflicted one; he has not hidden his face from him but has listened to his cry for help.

PSALM 22:24

Dear Great Physician, my child is sick and I am growing weary in faith and physical stamina. Please forgive me for doubting that you are able to do all things— even heal the sick. The demands of caring for an ill child leave me tired and full of self-pity. Father, I don't want my child to feel like he is a burden for me. Help me to be patient and loving, and forgive me when I doubt your wisdom and power to heal.

REFLECTION: Are there times when you are so overwhelmed in caring for your child that you doubt God's ability to heal—physically, emotionally or spiritually? Give those situations to God and trust him to work in his time. Our hope is in the Lord.

Thanksgiving

When you pass through the waters, I will be with you;
and when you pass through the rivers, they will not sweep over you.
When you walk through the fire, you will not be burned;
the flames will not set you ablaze.
For I am the LORD, your God, the Holy One of Israel, your Savior.

ISAIAH 43:2–3

Thank you, Heavenly Father for personally being with me
in every trial and in every hard place.
That truth brings incredible comfort to my heart.
I am grateful for the reminder that it's not "if"
I pass through hard times, but "when" I pass through them.
My faith does not exempt my children or me from sickness.
Through your grace I can take my eyes off my difficulties
and focus on you. You are forever worthy of my trust. I am blessed.

Continued Thanks

God tells us to give thanks in all things. What waters are you passing through today? Will you choose to thank God for them? Trust him; his plan is perfect. He will see you through.

Intercession

Be strong and courageous, Do not be terrified; do not be discouraged, for the LORD your God will be with you wherever you go.

JOSHUA 1:9

Oh Lord, my healer, I pray for my child to be strong and courageous, and not terrified or discouraged with the illness he is facing. Please be with him wherever he goes and provide your strength as he fights daily challenges. I long for the time when he will enjoy good health. I pray for your healing power to touch my child's body. During this time of sickness, I pray that you will strengthen my child's inner spirit. I pray that his sickness will make him a more compassionate, caring person, one who is quick to pray for others who are sick. I pray for the doctors and ask you to grant them wisdom, understanding, and compassion in treating my child. Please help my child to sleep peacefully knowing that you are with him and will never forsake him. In Jesus' name, Amen.

Continued Intercession

Ask God to help your child learn to comfort others with the same comfort he has received from God (2 CORINTHIANS 1:3-4).
Pray for him not lose heart (2 CORINTHIANS 4:16).
Pray your child is not fearful because God is with him (PSALM 23:4).

God's Promise for Your Child

I am the LORD, your God, who takes hold of your right hand and says to you, Do not fear; I will help you.

ISAIAH 41:13

Trusting the Great Physician

At fifteen, my son's future looked so promising. Academically, he was ranked eleventh in his class. Athletically, he was sought after as a cross-country runner, and had hopes of a full scholarship to the college of his choice.

Then came the dark and awful cloud, grande mal seizures that would forever change his life and ours. A medical nightmare soon followed with a drug regimen that adversely affected everything about our bright and gifted son. For a year and a half he "checked out" of life, and was lost on every front—mind, body, soul. We hardly recognized him.

Desperate for help, we prayed. We asked others to pray, and we had the elders in our fellowship pray over him, anointing him with oil. At one point we decided to take him off the drugs that caused such hostile and unpleasant reactions. Our good intention resulted in two more seizures and a hospital stay. We struggled with feelings of hopelessness, but we never stopped praying. We continued to plead with God for our son's healing.

Today we are still praying, still pleading on our knees. However, we have come to understand what has sustained us. We have NOT lost our trust, and we know exactly where to place it. Not in the medical community—not in the drugs or therapy, not even in prayer itself. We place our trust in God alone. We are counting on his character. We're convinced that a faithful God cannot be unfaithful because that goes against his very nature.

Years of pouring out our hearts for this boy have had an amazing outcome. It has pushed us below the surface of superficial faith. We've been submerged to the depths of God's love and have experienced his character. Our God is the Great Physician, and we rest in that knowledge.

Mom, I Need Safety and Protection

PRAISE GOD BECAUSE HE IS MY STRONGHOLD

The LORD is my light and my salvation –
whom shall I fear?
The LORD is the stronghold of my life –
of whom shall I be afraid?

PSALM 27:1

Lord, with delight I acknowledge that you are my stronghold —
your very presence is my protection. You are my sure shelter and reliable refuge.
The storms of life will come, but I am safe within the impenetrable walls
of your stronghold. You are the safe place for me and my family.
Hallelujah.

CONTINUED PRAISE

God is a Stronghold from those who might harm me (2 SAMUEL 22:3).
God is a fortress where I can run and be safe (PROVERBS 18:10).
God is my hiding place (PSALM 32:7).
God is a secure dwelling place (PSALM 27:5).

Confession

I acknowledged my sin to you and did not cover up my iniquity.
I said "I will confess my transgressions to the LORD" –
and you forgave the guilt of my sin.

PSALM 32:5

My Loving God, forgive me for attempting to cover up my sins.
My hiding has been futile and has left me miserable,
feeling far from you, and vulnerable.
I long for the comfort and security of your presence again.
Thank you for forgiving me so that I can draw near to you
and enjoy restored fellowship.
I will lie down and sleep in peace, for you alone, O LORD,
make me dwell in safety (Psalm 4:8).

REFLECTION: Do you experience regret when you run from the stronghold of God's protection? What areas of your life do you try to cover up? Do not forget, guilt is gone when you confess.

THANKSGIVING

The name of the LORD is a strong tower;
the righteous run to it and are safe.

PROVERBS 18:10

God my Stronghold, I thank you for the personal
protection you give to my children and me.
You are a mighty fortress, a strong tower,
whose walls cannot be penetrated or destroyed.
No enemy can touch my children or me
when we are safe within your arms.
This truth gives me sweet peace during those times
when I am afraid, exhausted, and in need of a hiding place.
I sing a song of thanks
for I have no fear as I abide in you.

CONTINUED THANKS

Reflect on the specific ways you have experienced God's protection in your life and in the life of your family. Take time to thank God, your protector.

INTERCESSION

I will take refuge in the shadow of your wings, O LORD,
until the disaster has passed.

PSALM 57:1

Dear Lord my Protector, I pray that my child will take refuge in the shadow of your wings until the disaster has passed. You know the circumstances and situations, the places and people that cause my child to feel at risk. I trust you, Lord, to meet my child at the center of these fearful places and situations. Spread your wings, Lord, and cover and protect my dear child. In Jesus name, Amen.

CONTINUED INTERCESSION

Ask God to keep your child from all harm (PSALM 121:7–8).
Ask God to clothe her with spiritual armor (EPHESIANS 6:11–18).
Pray she will be assured and safe in God's presence (PROVERBS 18:10).

GOD'S PROMISE TO YOUR CHILD

Let your child who belongs to the LORD rest secure in him, for he shields her all day long, the one the LORD loves, rests between his shoulders.

DEUTERONOMY 33:12, AUTHOR'S PARAPHRASE

An Angel in Yellow

My daughter, Laura, gave her heart to Jesus at age three. However, as a teen she decided being a Christian wasn't for her. Even so, Jesus has never given up and has kept his hand on her life despite her efforts to stray.

When she was eighteen, she traveled out of state to visit a friend. While there, the two of them went to a concert. Laura and I had discussed this particular band many times before. I agreed with her that they had a great sound, but their lyrics were especially offensive and blatantly anti-Jesus.

By a fluke, I learned that my daughter and her friend were on their way to this concert. From 700 miles away, there was little I could do to stop her. But I could pray.

That morning I talked to a woman who at one time had a wayward son. She said she used to pray, "Lord, send an angel to watch over him." Although I was skeptical, I prayed that prayer for Laura.

The next day I picked her up from the airport and asked her about the concert. She told me her eyes were opened to evil. "It was both beautiful and compelling, repulsive and horrifying," she said. Then she added, "This might sound weird, but I think the lead singer sold his soul to the devil. Do you think that's possible?"

We had a great discussion about that. Then she told me about a man wearing a bright yellow shirt with 'Jesus' on it who stood next to her during the entire concert. "He just stood there, not saying anything. Who wears a yellow Jesus shirt to a concert?" she asked. My heart pounded. An angel would, I thought. I don't know if the man was really an angel. But he was an answer to my prayer, if only to remind me that wherever my daughter goes, Jesus goes with her. That thought comforts me. Someday I pray it will comfort Laura, too.

Mom, I Need to Feel Accepted

PRAISE GOD BECAUSE JESUS IS HIS BELOVED

Praise be to the God and Father of our Lord Jesus Christ,
who has blessed us in the heavenly realms
with every spiritual blessing in Christ.
For he chose us in him before the creation of the world
to be holy and blameless in his sight.

EPHESIANS 1:3–4

Praise be to God! You chose me to be your child before the world began. You treat me with the same love as you do your beloved son, Jesus. It is as if you opened the windows of heaven announcing your high and holy love for your son and me. He is your holy perfect Son who brings you great joy and pleasure. The name "Beloved" so perfectly expresses your relationship with your Son whom you love for all of eternity. Thank you for sharing so great a love with me.

CONTINUED PRAISE

Jesus is his Beloved Son (MATTHEW 17:5).
God chose us to be his child (JOHN 15:16).
We are accepted in the Beloved (EPHESIANS 1:5–7).

CONFESSION

Restore to me the joy of your salvation, O LORD,
and grant me a willing spirit, to sustain me.

PSALM 51:12

Loving Lord, my heart seems far from your love. I have neglected the reading
of your word and prayer, causing me to feel far from you. Forgive me for
allowing the distance between us. I know I'm the one who moved—not you.
I want to draw near to you. I so crave your warm embrace of love and
acceptance once again. Restore to me the joy of my salvation.

REFLECTION: Confess those things that have kept you at a distance
from your Beloved Savior. God's forgiveness will free you to draw closer to
him. He longs to reveal his love to you.

Thanksgiving

To all who received Christ, to those who believed in his name,
he gave the right to become children of God.

John 1:12

Dear Father, I am overwhelmed with gratitude to be called beloved just as you call Jesus beloved. I sincerely thank you with all my heart for choosing me and saving me from all my sin through the blood of Jesus. By that one act I can stand before you holy as your beloved child. It is more than my mind can comprehend. It makes me feel so special to know that you wanted me. There is absolutely nothing greater than the realization that I belong to you. Thank you that I am your beloved child.

Continued Thanks

Let the words of the Jesus make you feel treasured and wanted:
My sheep listen to my voice; I know them, and they follow me.
I give them eternal life, and they shall never perish;
no one can snatch them out of my hand.
My Father, who has given them to me, is greater than all;
no one can snatch them out of my Father's hand.

John 10:27–30

INTERCESSION

God has made us accepted in the Beloved.

EPHESIANS 1:6 NKJV

Dear gracious Father, I ask that my child will know that by your grace, she has been accepted in Jesus, your beloved son. Lord, it tears my heart apart to see my child feeling rejected, insecure, and unloved. She often says, "I'm never going to be good enough. Why would anyone want to like me?" I ask that she will know how much you love her. Jesus, you loved her so much that you gave your life for her — there is no greater love than that. Deliver her from any doubts concerning this truth. I pray my child will believe with her heart, not just her mind, that you love her completely. May she find significance and acceptance because she is your beloved. In Jesus' name, Amen.

CONTINUED INTERCESSION

Pray for peace in your child's heart, and the knowledge of God's love for her
(1 JOHN 4:9–10).

Pray that she abides in Jesus' love (JOHN 15:9–10).

Pray that she meditates on God's unfailing love for her (PSALM 119:76; 143:8).

GOD'S PROMISE FOR YOUR CHILD

*The Spirit himself testifies with our spirit that we are God's children.
Now if we are children, then we are heirs—
heirs of God and co-heirs with Christ, if indeed we share in his sufferings
in order that we may also share in his glory.*

ROMANS 8:16–17

The Morning Blessing

My daughter Lisa's school days in special education were a battle for both of us. I saw the sadness reflected in her eyes each day as I dropped her off at school. She would look back, beckoning me with unspoken words, "Mommy, don't leave me here, take me home where I feel safe."

The world of special education can feel foreign and dangerous to a child. Each day, my heart beat with a prayer that she would feel accepted in Jesus. I longed for her to see herself as God saw her— beautiful and unique. When a prayer partner shared how she used Isaiah 61:3 as a visual prayer model, I adopted it for Lisa. I prayed that she would have a crown of beauty instead of ashes, the oil of gladness instead of mourning, the garment of praise instead of a spirit of despair.

I also started to do a morning blessing that added touch to my prayer. Every morning in the car, I molded my hands into the shape of a crown over Lisa's head. Then I lovingly rubbed her arms, signifying the oil of gladness. At last my arms encircled her in a tender embrace symbolizing the garment of praise. This daily ritual never failed to bring a smile to Lisa's face.

Some days were harder for Lisa than others. But I would remind Lisa that no matter what anyone said, she was a princess, the daughter of the King. This knowledge provided a safe place for her in an unpredictable environment.

The blessing came back to me as Lisa began to pray for me in my disappointing or frustrating moments. She would encircle my head with her hands, rub my arms vigorously and envelop me in her hearty hug. In those holy moments, my child would remind me that we were both daughters of the King.

Accepted in Jesus is a lovely place to live. Just ask Lisa and me. We still remind each other every morning.

Mom, I Need Good Friends

PRAISE JESUS BECAUSE HE IS MY FRIEND

*Jesus said, "Greater love has no one than this,
that he lay down his life for his friends."*

JOHN 15:13

*Lord Jesus, you are truly the best friend I have.
Your friendship is unequaled. I honor you and am forever grateful
to you for laying down your life for me at the cross
and purchasing my salvation. There is no greater love than that.
You declared friendship to a world that was hostile toward you.
What a display of unconditional love and friendship.*

CONTINUED PRAISE

Jesus is your intimate friend (JOHN 15:15).
Jesus is a loyal friend (HEBREWS 13:5).
Jesus is a friend who loves at all times (PROVERBS 17:17).
Jesus is a faithful friend (1 CORINTHIANS 1:9)

CONFESSION

*Whoever loves his brother lives in the light and there is nothing in him
to make him stumble. But whoever hates his brother is in the darkness
and walks around in the darkness; he does not know where he is going,
because the darkness has blinded him.*

1 JOHN 2:10–11

*Dear Father, I long to have my heart cleansed from the hateful emotions
that I cling to in difficult relationships. I see that by withholding love from
others I have stepped out of your light. I ask your forgiveness for wanting to
cause pain to others. It is only by your love and grace that my trespasses are
forgiven; help me to forgive others of theirs.*

REFLECTION: Do you have friendships that need to be restored? Are you
holding a grudge? Is your heart growing bitter? Do you need to ask forgiveness
of someone? Feel the cleansing of the Holy Spirit as you obey his voice.

Thanksgiving

I no longer call you servants,
because a servant does not know his master's business.
Instead, I have called you friends,
for everything that I learned from my Father
I have made known to you.

JOHN 15:15

Loving Jesus, how grateful I am for your perfect friendship
that is displayed by your death on a sinner's cross.
My heart rejoices that you call me friend and share with me
all the Father has made known to you.
What joy to know that your friendship means
your total loyalty, care, and constant presence.
Thank you for filling my lonely heart and being my friend forever.

Continued Thanks

In what ways has Jesus been a friend to you? Reflect on the many ways he shows you his friendship. How does his friendship make you feel?

Intercession

He who walks with the wise grows wise,
but a companion of fools suffers harm.

PROVERBS 13:20

Dear Jesus, I ask you to help my child to walk with the wise so he grows wise. Protect him from being a companion of fools so he won't suffer harm. Help my child to be cautious in choosing his friends. May he come to understand that the foundation of friendship is unconditional love — the kind of love you have for him. Please provide at least one Christian friend for my child so that together they can encourage one another's faith, be strong in godly character, and make godly decisions. I also pray for the salvation of his friends. In Jesus' name, Amen

Continued Intercession

Pray your child's love for his best friend, Jesus, grows deep
(EPHESIANS 3:16–19).
Ask God to help your child to know the value of friends
(ECCLESIASTES 4:9–10).
Pray for your child to be a forgiving friend (PROVERBS 17:9).
Ask God to help your child be a witness to his unsaved friends (1 PETER 3:15).

God's Promise for Your Child

Jesus said, "You are my friends if you do what I command."

JOHN 15:14

You've Got a Friend

David, our third-born, is shy and reserved. While his siblings canvased the neighborhood looking for playmates, this quiet seven-year-old was usually home alone building wonderful contraptions with Legos. Although he never said so, I sensed he wanted a special friend. My prayer for my little Lego-builder was that the Lord would give him a like-minded companion.

The following school year was one of answered prayer for David. He met Sam, a boy in his class. In God's providence, I already knew Sam's mom—I prayed with her weekly at Moms In Touch. Desiring to see this relationship develop, I invited Sam to play at our house one day after school.

As the boys settled into the back seat of my van, I watched David squirming as he tried to rouse the courage to speak. Then his nervous sentences came out in stutters. As he lowered his eyes and shut his mouth, his lip trembled a little. It was then that I heard God speak through David's new buddy.

"Go ahead!" Sam said. "I'm listening … tell me what you were gonna say." These simple words fastened two youngsters into a friendship that became enduring. They were inseparable.

Sometime later we had to present the unwelcome news to our kids of a possible move. My reticent David was the first to speak. "I don't make friends easily, Mom. When you prayed, that got better. If we move, can I ask you one thing?"

This mature linking of our prayer and the answer to it with Sam's new friendship touched my heart. At that moment, David could have asked for almost anything.

"And what would that be, David?"

His eyes crinkled as he smiled. "If we move, you have to join a Moms In Touch group right away. Promise?"

I smiled back, a grin that started in my heart. "Oh, David. That's a promise!"

Mom, I Need to Learn How to Forgive

PRAISE JESUS BECAUSE OF HIS GRACE

In Christ we have redemption through his blood, the forgiveness of sins,
in accordance with the riches of God's grace
that he lavished on us with all wisdom and understanding.

EPHESIANS 1:7

Lord, with loving reverence I worship you for your grace, grace that pardons and cleanses me from all my sin and guilt. Your grace is nothing less than the boundless love you expressed in the gift of your Son, Jesus. It is through grace I have been forgiven. I did nothing to earn it or deserve it. O Lord, I exalt you for your infinite, forgiving grace – freely given to all who believe. Amazing grace. How sweet the sound.

CONTINUED PRAISE

God's grace is abundant (ROMANS 5:17, 20).
God's grace is sufficient for all our needs (2 CORINTHIANS 12:9).
Through God we have eternal grace (2 TIMOTHY 1:9).

CONFESSION

Repent and turn to God, so that your sins may be wiped out,
that times of refreshing may come from the Lord,
and that he may send the Christ,
who has been appointed for you—even Jesus.

ACTS 3:19–20

Dear Lord, I confess my bitterness and retaliation toward one who has hurt me deeply. I admit I have not extended to him the same forgiveness you give me every time I sin. You immediately forgive and don't hold ill thoughts toward me, but I wait in judgment for my offender to make the same mistake again. I am so sorry for my tendency to hold grudges. These are harmful habits, and they put me in a prison of my own making. I want my relationship with you and with others to be right, so I am choosing to repent.

REFLECTION: As you wait in God's presence, ask him to reveal to you people that you still need to forgive. Pour out your thoughts and feelings. Now set your mind on Jesus and meditate on the way he forgives you. Delight in the freedom of forgiving others and the refreshment it brings to your soul.

THANKSGIVING

God is able to make all grace abound to you, so that in all things at all times, having all that you need, you will abound in every good work.

2 CORINTHIANS 9:8

Dear Father, I thank you so much for your saving grace, the grace that gives me strength to live a life pleasing to you. When I need to forgive, you give me a merciful attitude. You help me remember all the sins you have forgiven me, making it easier for me to forgive others for their small offenses against me. Thank you for your unlimited all-sufficient grace.

CONTINUED THANKS

Thank Jesus for his example of forgiveness and all encompassing grace when he said, "Father forgive them, for they do not know what they are doing" (Luke 23:34). When he died, he died also for the sins others have committed against you.

Intercession

Be kind and compassionate to one another,
forgiving each other, just as in Christ God forgave you.

Ephesians 4:32

Gracious Father, I pray for my child to be kind and compassionate to others, forgiving them just as God forgave her. She is having a hard time forgiving someone. She has been deeply hurt and is holding a grudge. I ask you to replace the spirit of bitterness with the spirit of forgiveness. May she extend that same grace to the one who has offended her. I ask that your grace will abound in her life, giving her strength to rid herself of resentment. May she experience victory and freedom — the fruit of forgiveness. In Jesus' precious name I pray, Amen.

Continued Intercession

Pray your child will not return evil for evil, but instead respond with a blessing
(1 Peter 3:9).
Pray she will obey God's command to forgive (Matthew 18:21–22).
Pray that she intercedes for those who have mistreated her (Luke 6:28).
Pray that she will overlook an offense (Proverbs 19:11).

God's Promise for your Child

When you stand praying, if you hold anything against anyone,
forgive him, so that your Father in heaven may forgive you your sins.

Matthew 6:14

STOP THE PAIN

Annie knew the young man liked her, but he made her nervous. My thirteen-year-old daughter confided that this unwelcome suitor intimidated her. "He is just too much, Mom!"

Annie shivered a bit as we talked and I sensed a crisis in the making. The boy's inappropriate comments continued, and he grew bolder with each encounter. At first Annie tried to make light of it. But when physical advances accompanied the boy's rude comments, we knew it was time to act. My husband and I encouraged Annie to confront the boy and ask him to "cease and desist."

Annie knew this was the right thing to do, but she dreaded what might happen afterwards. If only she could avoid him and his friends. But that was not an option as they were in several of her classes. As a mom, it was painful to see my Annie struggle through such an awkward experience, one that she had neither provoked nor encouraged. My heart wanted to rescue her, but I thought better of it. Instead, I determined to be her safe haven.

The day arrived when this young man crossed one too many lines. On the way to class, he grabbed Annie from behind, startling and embarrassing her with his brash forwardness. She knew she would have to report the incident, but she feared the consequences when her classmate discovered that she was the informant.

Even now my eyes fill with tears as I recall the anguish this experience caused my beautiful daughter. She felt violated and crushed. Annie and I prayed together, and she agreed to allow me to join her when she met with the school counselor. I prayed silently and listened with admiration as she told her story with bold composure. The counselor understood the gravity of the situation, and the young man was suspended from school. When he finally returned, Annie kept her distance. He apologized and respected her space.

But wounds of this nature linger. We waited for the turbulence to settle, and soon we saw courageous resolve return to Annie's countenance. Jesus would forgive and she would, too.

Mom, I Want to Honor My Parents

PRAISE JESUS BECAUSE OF HIS FATHERHOOD

"I will be a Father to you, and you will be my
sons and daughters," says the Lord Almighty.

2 CORINTHIANS 6:18

Dear God, how very special is the Fatherhood of God— it is of great value and significance, for it is the way you desire your creation to relate to you. I magnify your name and bless you, dear Father, that you want this kind of relationship with me. I rejoice that as creator you have authority over all the heavens and the earth. I praise you that as your offspring, I have the privilege of being under your authority and have access to your unlimited wisdom, vast resources and boundless love. I celebrate the truth that I belong to you — my Father.

CONTINUED THANKS

God is your creator and provider (1CORINTHIANS 8:6; ACTS 17:24–28).

God is a compassionate Father (PSALM 103:13; I JOHN 3:1–2).

God disciplines those he loves (HEBREWS 12:5-6; PROVERBS 3:11–12).

109

CONFESSION

Walk in all the way that the LORD your God has commanded you so that you may live and prosper and prolong your days in the land that you will possess.

DEUTERONOMY 5:33

Dear Father, forgive me for not wanting to walk in all your ways. I know your commands for me are always for my good, and yet I find myself choosing to go my own way. I so want to please you, but there are many times I do not. Please give me the strength to live according to your Word. In Jesus' name I pray, Amen.

REFLECTION: What are the influences that cause you to wander away from God's direction and guidance? Are there times you dishonor God? Trust God to help you do better in the future. Anticipate the peace, security and happiness that will come as a result of obedience.

Thanksgiving

The LORD tends his flock like a shepherd:
He gathers the lambs in his arms
and carries them close to his heart;
he gently leads those that have young.

ISAIAH 40:11

Father, I love the thought of you as my father and shepherd.
I thank you for the image given in Isaiah
of you gathering your children, all your children,
young and old, in your arms and holding them close,
making them feel loved and secure.
I especially thank you for those times when I feel tired and weary
and you carry me right where I can nestle close to your heart.
I am so appreciative of your gentleness with me
as you lead me and give me the wisdom I need.
What an awesome Father you are.
Thank you for making me feel loved and accepted.

CONTINUED THANKS

When have you felt carried by your heavenly Father? Daily? Have you thanked him?

INTERCESSION

Paul wrote: Children, obey your parents in the Lord, for this is right.
"Honor your father and mother"—
which is the first commandment with a promise—
"that it may go well with you and that you may enjoy long life on the earth".

EPHESIANS 6:1–2

Heavenly Father, my hope for my child is that he will obey his father and I as his parents, for this is right. May he honor his father and myself so that it may go well with him and he enjoys long life on this earth. Please give him an eager and willing heart open to taking guidance and direction from us. Help him to see that as your chosen representatives we are responsible to lead, guide and give him direction in the way he should go. Help us to be good examples of what is right and good. Grant us wisdom and the love needed to confront our child with respect. May he heed our instruction and discipline. Please give him a heart that wants to please you, his Father. In Jesus' name, Amen.

CONTINUED INTERCESSION

Ask God to help your child understand the blessings of honoring his parents
(COLOSSIANS 3:20).
Pray that your child will listen and learn from you (PROVERBS 1:8–9).
Pray for your child to show proper respect to everyone (I PETER 2:17).

GOD'S PROMISE FOR YOUR CHILD

Honor your father and your mother, as the LORD your God has commanded you, so that you may live long and that it may go well with you in the land the LORD your God is giving you.

DEUTERONOMY 5:16

FATHER KNOWS BEST

It was the summer of 1971. I was a year out of high school and quite certain I was ready to be an adult. I lived under the assumption that my graduation cap and gown were my ticket to maturity. Finished were the days of needing parental advice. Dad's counsel, once respected and honored, was now irritating, especially when it came to riding motorcycles.

That summer, Billy Wigham invited me to go for a ride with him on his Harley. I'd never been a passenger on a motorcycle before and I found the thought of it exciting. I felt brave, adventurous and a little naughty. Had it stopped with a casual ride, my disobedience would have remained a minor infraction. But I elevated my reckless act into a capital offense — I drove the Harley and I crashed the Harley.

Somehow I confused the brake and the clutch and the three of us ended up in a country ditch: Billy, me, and Harley. At first the pain was more emotional, but hours later it became physical as I identified slivers and thistles lodged in every square inch of my bare arms.

I told no one and tried bear the growing pain in my arms. My secret was safe ... until the night following my mishap. Unable to stand the pain any longer, I called Dr. Beebe. He met me at his office, and for the next hour he worked dozens of stickers out of my swelling arms. My tears flowed as I gritted my teeth and breathed hard, knowing that the pain wouldn't end when Dr. Beebe finished. I still had to go home and face the music, and I knew I wouldn't like the tune.

That evening was a blur of emotions. It was the last time I can recall saying something disrespectful and cruel to my father. Three decades later I still wince as I remember the volatile exchange. "You can't tell me what to do! I will do what I want and if you don't like it, I will move out of this house!" I spit out the words with a fury that shocked my dad. He did something he had never done before and never repeated. He slapped my face.

We were both devastated and broken. We fell into each other's arms with sobs of remorse and repentance.

My dad was a good man, a regular guy who loved me, protected me, and prayed for me. He passed on this prayer legacy and I am passing it on to my child. Father Knows Best was a favorite TV series during the early 60s. It was a good title then and a good principle to live by now.

Mom, I Need Help Resisting Peer Pressure

PRAISE GOD BECAUSE HE IS VICTORIOUS

To God belong strength and victory.

JOB 21:31

Dear Almighty God, I praise you that victory belongs to you. From your Sovereign throne the view is always victorious, for you are the ultimate Victor. Nothing can stand against you. So great is your power that your enemies cringe before you (Psalm 66:3). I praise you for you are my God of eternal triumph. Your Presence is victory — I will not be shaken by the people around me. Blessed are all who take refuge in you, victorious God.

CONTINUED PRAISE

God is the source of all victory (DEUTERONOMY 20:1–4).

Victory is by God alone (PSALM 20:7–8).

Through Jesus we have victory over evil (GENESIS 3:15; REVELATION 15:2).

CONFESSION

Live by the Spirit, and you will not gratify
the desires of the sinful nature.
For the sinful nature desires what is contrary to the Spirit,
and the Spirit what is contrary to the sinful nature.
They are in conflict with each other,
so that you do not do what you want.

GALATIANS 5:16–17

Dear Lord, I am so disappointed and frustrated
when I do those things that I know displease you.
I lose my joy and feel defeated.
Forgive me for following the ways
and people of the world instead of you.
Help me not to be lead astray by false values.
I am sorry for my selfishness and pride.
Fill me with your Holy Spirit and help me keep a pure heart.

REFLECTION: Think of the people in your life who have the most influence over you—your family, your friends, your church family, even celebrities. Are they wise or foolish? Ask God to help you discern the words of the wise and shut out the other voices.

Thanksgiving

Jesus said, "In this world you will have trouble.
But take heart! I have overcome the world."

John 16:33

Dear Heavenly Father,
because Jesus overcame the world, I can, too.
Thank you for your Word that enables me
to hear your voice of truth every day and for the power
of the Holy Spirit that enables me to resist lies,
the ways of the foolish, and pressure to do wrong.
You have blessed me with wise, godly people in my life.
Thank you for your encouragement to do right.
I am deeply thankful for your constant wisdom and guidance.
Thank you for the promise that the power of the living Christ
within me has not only given me victory over death,
but also victory over sin and temptation.

Continued Thanks

Can you think of times when God has helped you discover evil in people and resist it? Thank him for the victories.

Intercession

Dear children, do not let anyone lead you astray.
He who does what is right is righteous, just as God is righteous.

1 John 3:7

Dear Father, hear my prayers for my child. I ask that no one will lead him astray. I pray that he will do what is righteous just as you are righteous. Give him discernment in his choice of friends. I pray that he will not join the company of those who are bent on disobedience. May he influence them, but not be open to their influence. Father, he faces so much pressure from his peers. Help him to be strong in his convictions and courageous to stand alone, even if it means losing a friend. I ask you to give him your strength so he will be bold in the face of opposition. I pray that he will be victorious in his faith by choosing to follow Jesus. In Jesus' name, Amen.

Continued Intercession

Pray that your child does not conform to the world (Romans 12:1–2).
Pray that your child is able to resist peer pressure (Proverbs 1:10; 4:14;
Exodus 23:2; 2 Timothy 2:22).

God's Promise for Your Child

I will give you words and wisdom that none of your adversaries
will be able to resist or contradict. You will be betrayed even by parents,
brothers, relatives and friends …All men will hate you because of me.
But not a hair of your head will perish. By standing firm you will gain life.

Luke 21:15–19

Mighty Men

From day one, Max kept me on my knees. My precious son's learning disabilities had made education a real challenge for him and constant concern for his dad and me. Max was my reason to pray with a Moms In Touch group.

As we prepared for Max to enter high school, I cautiously observed the resource classes he would be attending. What I saw there was sobering and chilling. The peers that Max would rub shoulders with were troubled, angry teens with attitudes and appearances suggesting little moral or spiritual foundation. How could I place my son in this negative environment?

That summer I was filled with anxious thoughts about Max's first year in high school. But my Bible study plan for August took me to a similar circumstance. As I read the story of David in 1 Samuel 22, I followed him into the caves where he hid, hoping to escape King Saul's plot to murder him. I examined David's peer group— 400 malcontents. They were men in distress, men in debt, and men who were angry and ready to explode. But the Scriptures call these outlaws David's "Mighty Men," because they were transformed and empowered by his leadership.

As I finished the story, I sensed the Lord speaking to my troubled heart, "If I am able to care for David in the midst of 400 rebels, I can protect Max in a classroom of 20." My heart lightened and my spirits lifted.

Our circumstances are never a surprise to our God, for he is able. He could protect and use my son, even in this situation. King David was testimony to this truth: God had done it before. He could do it again for my Max.

Mom, I Need Someone Special to Look Up to

PRAISE GOD BECAUSE HE IS MY HEAVENLY FATHER

"I will be a Father to you, and you will be my sons and daughters, says the Lord Almighty."

2 CORINTHIANS 6:18

Heavenly Father, I exalt your name— you are my Father and I praise you. "Father" is the attribute that speaks of a close and intimate relationship. What an honor it is for me to call you Father. As your daughter I rejoice in your infinite love, your boundless mercy that saves me, your words that nourish me, your faithfulness in meeting my needs, your wisdom that guides me, and your comforting Presence. My Father, I look up to you and cherish you.

CONTINUED PRAISE

God is a loving and compassionate Father (PSALM 103:13).
Your Father created you (ISAIAH 64:8).
You can know your Father through his Son (JOHN 14:6).

119

CONFESSION

Since, then, you have been raised with Christ,
set your hearts on things above,
where Christ is seated at the right hand of God.
Set your minds on things above, not on earthly things.

COLOSSIANS 3:1–2

Dear Father, please forgive me for doubting that you will take care of me.
I am caught up with the worries of life — at times they strangle me.
There are so many people in the world whose words sound true but aren't,
and I'm tempted to look and follow them. Please help me to discern
who has your Spirit and speaks your words and who doesn't.
Calm my anxious heart long enough to remember your words,
reminding me of how valuable I am to you.
Forgive me when I turn away from your love and purpose in my life.

REFLECTION: Ask God, your Father, to show you where you are following man-made thoughts and traditions rather than God. Commit to studying God's Word so you can tell the difference. Read Psalm 103:17–18 and hear God's promise of love for you when you obey his precepts.

Thanksgiving

How great is the love the Father has lavished on us,
that we should be called children of God.

1 JOHN 3:1

My God, I am so thankful that you are my Father and you sent
your Son to be the perfect example for my children and me.
I am abundantly blessed by all the fatherly things that you do for me.
I love how you care about every little thing in my life.
You always listen to me, comfort me when I'm sad, and guide me
when I am confused and overwhelmed.
Thank you for the times you have extended your hand to me
by sending someone at just the precise moment I needed help.
You know what my needs are even before I ask you.
You are a Father I can count on, a Father I can trust. I love you.

Continued Thanks

Reflect on the character of Jesus—his love, his compassion, his mercy, his courage, his strength, and his submission before the Father. Now think of what a loving, kind and compassionate Father God is to all his children.

Intercession

Jesus said, "I am the light of the world. Whoever follows me will never walk in darkness, but will have the light of life."

John 8:12

My Precious Lord, thank you for your perfect Son, Jesus, who is the light of the world. He is the perfect light for my child to look up to and follow. I pray my child will let Jesus be the hero she so desperately needs so she never walks in darkness. May her heart long to be like you: kind, compassionate, honest, forgiving, and full of love. I pray that she chooses earthly role models who reflect your nature. May she pledge allegiance to you, her Lord and Savior, and take pride in being called your child. I pray that you will always be her number one role model. In Jesus' name, Amen.

Continued Intercession

Pray your child does not choose ungodly role models
(1Corinthians 5:11; 2 Corinthians 6:14).
Pray she recognizes that God is a Father to the Fatherless (Psalm 68:5).
Ask God to help your child follow only Jesus, not the teaching of men
(Colossians 2:8).

God's Promise for Your Child

You received the Spirit of sonship. And by him we cry, "Abba, Father." The Spirit testifies with our spirit that we are God's children.

Romans 8:15–16

The First Day

Hannah and her father were strangers with the same last name. He was seldom home and when he was, he was verbally abusive. It broke my heart and I worked hard to counter my husband's seeming inability to celebrate and affirm his daughter.

Weeks before Hannah left for college, she spilled her emotional pain, unloading a dump truck full of the hatred, anger, and resentment she felt toward her dad. I sobbed as I listened to the acid pain she had carried for too many years. It was at that moment I knew how to pray: "Lord, grant my precious daughter relationships that mirror your unconditional love for her. Give her friends, peers, and godly mentors she can look up to and follow."

My prayers were realized while Hannah attended college. Our phone visits became joyfully animated as she spoke of the godly friends the Lord was adding to her life: a compassionate and wise pastor, several nurturing professors, and kindred friends who were willing to journey with her. I shared her delight, but still detected the lingering sadness that she couldn't shake.

My prayers became more specific and more urgent. I asked the Lord to bring a godly man into her life, one who would love her without reservation, one who would protect and defend her and never shame her. I asked for a man who would hold her heart with grace-filled hands. I waited, knowing the Lord would answer in his perfect timing.

Hannah met Mike in her junior year. Mike loves Hannah the way God designed her; she is never required to earn his approval. Mike's compassion and acceptance are healing some of Hannah's deepest wounds. I have quietly watched her begin to trust again and to release some of the anger she holds toward her father. Hannah is even seeing her Heavenly Father through new eyes as she sees Mike's life mirror God's character.

Hannah graduated last May. In June, her father will walk her down the aisle and place her hand—and her life—in Mike's hand. My eyes will glisten with grateful tears as I celebrate the answers to my prayers. Hannah will begin the "first day of the rest of her life" with a man who will lead her and love her. But my heart still hurts because of one request that remains unanswered. So I will pray a new prayer—that the fruit of this covenant relationship with her husband will prompt a new beginning for Hannah and the first man in her life, her daddy.

Mom, I Want a Servant's Heart

PRAISE GOD BECAUSE JESUS IS A SERVANT

*"Here is my Servant, whom I uphold, my chosen one in whom I delight;
I will put my Spirit on him," says the Lord.*

ISAIAH 42:1

*Lord, as Sovereign God you became Servant. You descended from the highest
heaven, where you reigned in majesty and indescribable glory to become
human, Jesus Christ. I praise you for humbling yourself and coming to earth.
I adore you for leaving the splendor of heaven to take on man's limitations and
ultimate poverty. You came to serve and not be served. You did not pursue
your own interest, nor seek your own glory. There is no greater expression of
the love of God than the title of Christ as Servant.*

CONTINUED PRAISE

Praise God for the marvelous truth that he will one day exalt his servant Jesus
(PHILIPPIANS 2:4–8).

Jesus came to serve, not to be served (MATTHEW 20:26–28).

Christ did not seek his own glory (JOHN 8:50).

Christ was an obedient servant (HEBREWS 5:7–9; JOHN 8:29).

CONFESSION

Jesus said, "The greatest among you should be like the youngest,
and the one who rules like the one who serves."

LUKE 22:26

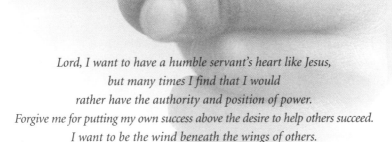

Lord, I want to have a humble servant's heart like Jesus,
but many times I find that I would
rather have the authority and position of power.
Forgive me for putting my own success above the desire to help others succeed.
I want to be the wind beneath the wings of others.
Help me to be more like Jesus.

REFLECTION: Do you seek external rewards? Is it important for others to see and appreciate your efforts? Are you afraid that people will take advantage of you? Repent of these attitudes and let the Holy Spirit cleanse you. You will then have the same attitude as Christ.

Thanksgiving

Jesus knew that the Father had put all things under his power,
and that he had come from God and was returning to God;
so he got up from the meal, took off his outer clothing, and wrapped
a towel around his waist. After that, he poured water into a basin
and began to wash his disciples' feet, drying them with
the towel that was wrapped around him.

John 13:3–5

Dear Lord, thank you for being the exemplary model of servanthood. Thank you for living a servant's life, caring and ministering to all those who needed your help. You turned no one away. I marvel at your goodness to others, but the greatest good was your sacrifice for the sins of the world. "Greater love has no one than this, that he lay down his life for his friends" (John 15:13). How can I give adequate thanks for this marvelous demonstration of servanthood? To God be the glory!

Continued Thanks

Meditate on the rest of the story of Jesus washing the disciples' feet in John 13:12–16. Verse 17 says that we will be happy if we follow his example. Give thanks that we can be genuinely excited about serving others.

Intercession

Each one should use whatever gift he has received
to serve others, faithfully administering
God's grace in its various forms.

1 PETER 4:10

Lord, help my child to use the gifts you have so generously given him to serve others. Teach him to do nothing out of selfish ambition or vain conceit, but humbly consider others before himself. Let him look not only on his own interests, but also to the interest of others. I ask that my child be sensitive to those around him. Allow him to rejoice when others succeed. I pray that he serves others with a humble attitude, not one of superiority. Help me to be a good example of your servant heart— a model he can follow. In Jesus' name I pray, Amen.

Continued Intercession

Pray that your child may have a humble and contrite heart (ISAIAH 66:2).
Pray that he honors others above himself (ROMANS 12:10).
Pray for your child to treat everyone equally (ROMANS 12:16).
Pray your child becomes a servant of the Lord (LUKE 1:38; JOHN 13:15–16).

God's Promise for Your Child

Humble yourselves before the Lord, and he will lift you up.

JAMES 4:10

Where's the Plunger?

Matt was not an easy child to raise. His high school years drained me, often exhausting even my passion to pray for him. It was in this time of raging emotions that my faithful prayer partners carried me above the storms that my son regularly stirred up. Then, in Matt's twenty-first year, God whispered and Matt heard. It was not a dramatic event, but it was a turning.

Always the free spirit, Matt had chosen to live away from home and work after high school rather than go to college right away. A year later he changed his mind and asked to return home to make it easier for him to earn money so he could further his education. My home had become a peaceful place, and I liked it that way. Even so, my husband and I agreed that this was the loving thing to do and we welcomed him home. When Matt returned, his behavior showed abundant evidence of answers to prayers of a lifetime. He was indeed a new creation.

Then one day the old Matt returned for a visit. He came charging down the stairs ranting hysterically, which raised the hair on the back of my neck. From his yelling, I wondered if we'd had a small earthquake and I had just missed it. But it was only a stopped-up toilet in need of a plunge job. Matt's response to my evaluation of the damage was classic. "Well, it's a mess, Mom, and somebody better clean it up!"

I reminded him that there were only two "somebodies" in the house and perhaps he was the chosen one. He shuffled, lowered his voice and said with more ownership and grace than I expected, "Oh, yeah. I guess I would be the man for the job." Glancing at the little puddles of water accumulating on the tile, he continued. "So, where did you say you keep the plunger?"

As I recall, not only did Matt unplug the toilet, but he also cleaned the whole bathroom. Later when I thanked him, he brushed the job off as though it was just a part of a good day's work. But I knew better. I had just seen the faint traces of a servant spirit being formed, fleshed out with a bathroom plunger and toilet scrubber.

Mom, I Need Courage

PRAISE GOD BECAUSE HE IS EVER-PRESENT

"Am I only a God nearby," declares the LORD,
"and not a God far away?
Can anyone hide in secret places
so that I cannot see him?"

JEREMIAH 23:23–24

Almighty God, I give you praise. There is no place that you are not. I am awestruck by the truth that your Presence encompasses all space. I worship and adore you, my God who is present with me every moment of my life. You always see me, know what is going on in my life, and are always there as my constant resource of courage and strength. Your constant presence in my life gives me the courage to live in a difficult world and to do what you have called me to do.

CONTINUED PRAISE

God promises to be present— always (JOSHUA 1:9; PSALM 139:1–3).
God knows and sees everything (PROVERBS 15:3).
God gives you the ability to do all things (PSALM 18:29).

CONFESSION

The eyes of the LORD range throughout the earth to strengthen those
whose hearts are fully committed to him.

2 CHRONICLES 16:9

My Ever-Present God,
I am not sure that my heart
is fully surrendered to you.
I want to be totally devoted to you,
but am swayed by the emotions of the moment.
At times you seem so distant that
I forget that you are always present.
Please help me to remember all the difficulties
you have brought me through
and draw courage from your power and promises.
Forgive me for not turning to you first.

REFLECTION: Think back and make a list of all the times God was there for you, helped you and gave you his courage to face difficulties. When you are tempted to panic, pull out your list and remember what God has done for you. He's there for you — take advantage of it.

Thanksgiving

Where can I go from your Spirit?
Where can I flee from your presence?
If I go up to the heavens, you are there;
if I make my bed in the depths, you are there.
If I rise on the wings of the dawn,
if I settle on the far side of the sea,
even there your hand will guide me,
your right hand will hold me fast.

Psalm 139:7–10

Lord, I am so thankful that you do not come and go in my life, but are always present. Every place life takes me I have a guide, a friend, a protector, a Father. Even though I can't see you, by faith I know that you are always with me. Thank you, my Almighty God, for your presence during the difficult times in my life. I can face tomorrow because you are holding my hand. I have great peace knowing that no matter where my children are or what they are experiencing you are with them as well. There's not a moment that they are out of your sight.

Continued Thanks

Tell God how grateful you are for his constant presence with your children. Can you think of a specific situation where you experienced God's presence? Acknowledge that he was there by giving thanks.

Intercession

"Be strong and courageous. Do not be terrified; do not be discouraged, for the Lord your God will be with you wherever you go."

Joshua 1:9

Father, I pray for my child to be strong and courageous, unafraid, nor discouraged. Let her know that the Lord her God is with her wherever she goes. I ask that you will help her face those things that cause panic in her heart. Give her courage to confront her mountains with confidence in the knowledge that through your strength she can and will succeed. Let her know your Presence is always with her, and help her look to you for courage to live according to your will. In Jesus' name, Amen.

Continued Intercession

Pray for your child that she will turn to Jesus when her courage is weak (Matthew 14:29–31).

Pray that her heart and mind are strengthened as she waits upon the Lord (Psalm 27:14; Isaiah 40:31).

Pray that she is firm in adverse circumstances (Ephesians 6:13).

God's Promise for Your Child

God is our refuge and strength,
an ever-present help in trouble.

Psalm 46:1

THE GIFT

Red flags went up in the Fall when our seventeen-year-old daughter, Lindy, began dating a college student. The young man was pleasant and polite, but we were uneasy with his lifestyle. Her dad and I expressed our concern, but we hit a barricade. When we suggested this relationship had the potential of compromising Lindy's spiritual, and possibly moral, standards, she put up thick walls.

Although Lindy would not be moved or persuaded by our words, we knew she could be moved by the power of our prayers. Talking to God about our concern brought immediate peace to our "parent panic" situation, even though we needed a fresh supply daily as we watched Lindy's resistance drag on.

For several months we prayed while Lindy made excuses to continue the relationship. Christmas vacation arrived and with it the answer to our prayers.

My husband and I had just gone to bed when Lindy burst into our bedroom, and spilled the news. "I did it! I just said it. It's over. I told him I couldn't live with myself when I felt I was lowering my standards because of our relationship."

As I peered into her eyes, I saw the resolution of a difficult choice made and celebrated. "How did he respond, Honey? Did he understand?"

Lindy looked away and there was a twinge of pain in her answer. "I don't think so, Mom, but it's OK. I know I did the right thing."

I could see the burden of the past several months beginning to slide off Lindy's shoulders. She squirmed off the bed and seemed to stand straighter, taller, and more confident. After goodnight kisses, she slipped out the door, then leaned back and whispered, "Thank you guys. Thanks, Mom, for praying that God would give me courage. You alone knew how much I needed that prayer!"

Lindy received a gift of courage as only the Father could give it. It was a very Merry Christmas, indeed.

Mom, I Need Patience

PRAISE GOD BECAUSE HE IS PATIENT

You, O LORD, are a compassionate and gracious God,
slow to anger, abounding in love and faithfulness.

PSALM 86:15

My Patient God, I declare with joy and adoration that patience is one of your divine attributes. You display patience through your great compassion and mercy. The power of your patience is gloriously demonstrated through your amazing kindness that leads us to repentance. I shout for joy when I think of the invincible, unwavering patience of Jesus. I celebrate your preeminent desire to reveal yourself, no matter how long it takes. I praise you for your patience.

CONTINUED PRAISE

God has unlimited patience (1 TIMOTHY 1:16).
God's anger lasts only a moment, his favor lasts a lifetime (PSALM 30:5; 78:38).
God imparts patience through the Holy Spirit
(ROMANS 15:5; GALATIANS 5:22–23).
God's patience leads to repentance (2 PETER 3:19, 15).

CONFESSION

A man's wisdom gives him patience,
it is to his glory to overlook an offense.

PROVERBS 19:11

My merciful Lord, forgive me for my impatience. I can get so irritated with
those I love the most. When I think about your patience with me, the offenses
of others seem so small and insignificant. I confess my agitation and anger
when things are not done to my liking or according to my timetable. Help
me to remember your loving patience with me and to demonstrate that love
by being patient with others.

REFLECTION: Ask the Holy Spirit to reveal to you the times you have
been impatient. What were the circumstances? Confess what the Spirit has
revealed. Tell God you are sorry and want to change. Experience the fruit of
his patience and go forward in the power of his Holy Spirit.

Thanksgiving

The Lord, the Lord, the compassionate and gracious God, slow to anger, abounding in love and faithfulness, maintaining love to thousands, and forgiving wickedness, rebellion and sin.

Exodus 34:6–7

Dear Jesus, I am truly thankful for your unlimited patience. I am thankful for your patience during the times I choose to exclude you from my life. Even then you are always waiting patiently for me to return. Gratefulness floods my heart when I consider that you refuse to give up on me. Sometimes I am a slow and stubborn student of life's lessons, but you continue to be my patient teacher and friend. What a blessing to know that your patience lasts a lifetime. Bless you, Father, that you also show unlimited patience to my children.

Continued Thanks

Meditate on those moments in your past where you felt God was orchestrating events to bring you one step closer to asking Christ into your life. As you ponder his loving patience, let your heart overflow with thanksgiving!

INTERCESSION

Be joyful in hope, patient in affliction, faithful in prayer.

ROMANS 12:12

Dear Faithful God, I ask that my child will be joyful in hope, patient in affliction and faithful in prayer. May he be strengthened with all power, great endurance, and patience according to your glorious might. Father, I know through the many times of trials and tests of life that patience comes with maturity. I know it is the testing of his faith that brings great endurance and greater faith. May he wait patiently, trusting your promises and obeying your word. Please give him a heart that perseveres. May he keep his eyes on you, the author and finisher of his faith. In Jesus' name, Amen.

CONTINUED INTERCESSION

Pray for your child to be patient as he waits to receive the promises of God (HEBREWS 6:12; 2 PETER 3:9).

Pray that your child clothes himself with patience (COLOSSIANS 3:12).

Pray that he will be patient and not quick-tempered (PROVERBS 14:29; 16:32).

GOD'S PROMISE FOR YOUR CHILD

I waited patiently for the LORD; he turned to me and heard my cry.

PSALM 40:1

HANDLE WITH CARE

My son's concept of time differs significantly from that of his clock-driven mother. I learned this early as Michael shuffled his way through his elementary school years. He was all too comfy with the consequences of tardiness and seldom considered them a crisis or worry.

I remember once when Michael had procrastinated and suddenly found himself faced with the deadline for his California Missions Map. The only evidence of his work was an angry collection of wadded paper in the wastebasket. With impatient fury, he destroyed the last remaining copies of what work he had completed. My own anger rose as I recalled coaching him the night before to slow down and take his time. With an empty homework folder tucked under his arm, fuming and stomping, Michael made his way to the door.

Accompanied by words that wounded, I pushed Michael out the screen door. His startled stare changed into a look of disgust that matched my own. As he slammed the gate, it was as if he slammed his heart shut as well.

The chilling sound reverberated loud and long as my eyes followed Michael's slight figure walking up the hill to his elementary school. I instantly regretted my impatience with him. I bowed my head and asked God to forgive me for my harsh, mean-spirited reaction. How could I be so impatient? The question that remained was, "Could I forgive myself?"

Moments later I was on campus, rushing to the door of Michael's 3rd grade classroom. I caught the teacher's eye, and she signaled Michael and motioned for him to meet me at the door. He walked toward me, eyes downcast. I spoke first. "Oh, Michael, Mom is so sorry. Can you forgive me for being so unkind and so impatient?" His smile was answer enough.

I had been hasty and intolerant, but Michael overlooked my behavior with a gracious hug. As I left Michael's classroom I realized that this had been a "teaching moment" for both of us, and many refresher courses would follow.

Life lessons can't be wrapped in packages marked "Rush." The label must read: "Handle with Care."

Mom, I Want to Control My Anger

PRAISE GOD BECAUSE HE IS MERCIFUL

Who is a God like you,
who pardons sin and forgives the transgression
of the remnant of his inheritance?
You do not stay angry forever, LORD, but delight to show mercy.

MICAH 7:18

Merciful Savior, there are times I deserve your wrath, instead you shower me with
your mercy. You give me an unlimited supply of second chances. I rejoice that your
mercy is extended to all of your creation and that it is new every single morning.
Oh, how I praise you that you delight in showing mercy instead of anger.

CONTINUED PRAISE

God has unlimited patience (1 TIMOTHY 1:16).
God's anger lasts only a moment, his favor last a lifetime
(PSALM 30:5; 78:38).
God imparts patience through the Holy Spirit (ROMANS 15:5).
God's patience leads to repentance (2 PETER 3:15, 19)

CONFESSION

In your anger do not sin:
Do not let the sun go down while you are still angry.
EPHESIANS 4:26

Dear Merciful Lord, I have not shown the kindness and mercy to others that
you show me. Too often my words are harsh and biting. I am quick to speak
and careless in my choice of words while you are slow to anger and very
compassionate. Forgive me for the ways I wound with angry words and
actions. Have mercy on me and take away my sin.

REFLECTION: As you open your heart to the Holy Spirit's gaze, what is
he revealing? Words and actions that may have wounded others? Continue
in an attitude of repentance and let the Lord guide you as you pray.

Thanksgiving

Be thankful. Let the word of Christ dwell in you richly as you
teach and admonish one another with all wisdom…
with gratitude in your hearts to God.

Colossians 3:15–16

Dear Father, I come with an offering of thanksgiving
because of your tender expressions of mercy and love.
Your words are kind and bring restoration;
they reflect the perfect balance of correction and mercy.
Jesus, I am so thankful for your story,
your "living biography" in Scripture.
Everything you did was laced with mercy and compassion.
I thank you that as your words sink deep into my heart,
I will be a conduit of your mercy, kindness, and love.

Continued Thanks

Ponder the ways Jesus has shown his mercy to you, granting you second
chances. Thank him for the wisdom, strength, and patience only he can
provide in times of anger. Thank him for empowering you to give second
chances to others.

Intercession

Everyone should be quick to listen, slow to speak and slow to become angry, for man's anger does not bring about the righteous life that God desires.

James 1:19–20

Loving, merciful Father, I pray my child will be quick to listen to what others have to say. Help him learn to be slow to speak and slow to become angry. Please help him not harbor anger, but be quick to resolve his conflicts so bitterness does not take root in his heart. Fill him with your wisdom so he will handle challenging situations in a loving and kind manner. Give him a heart of mercy and remind him that you have been merciful to him. In Jesus' name, Amen.

Continued Intercession

Pray that your child will not cling to his anger (Ephesians 4:26–27).
Pray your child is full of mercy (James 3:17).
Pray that your child's words will benefit others (Ephesians 4:29).
Pray your child will ask God for forgiveness when he rebels against him
(Daniel 9:9).

God's Promise for Your Child

"With everlasting kindness I will have compassion on you,"
say the Lord your Redeemer.

Isaiah 54:8

ANGRY WORDS

Angry words. Careless words. They are not uncommon for a busy young mother to utter without thinking. My mind flashes back to a Sunday morning many years ago when Brent, my only child, was four.

My husband and I directed music for a large church which made Sundays the week's most intense workday. Returning home after two services, I left Brent playing in the living room of our condo while I changed into casual clothes. As I unzipped my dress, I heard an alarming sound that sent me bolting into the adjacent room. What I saw filled me with shock—and rage. My son was creatively shredding an important music score for one of the choir pieces I was accompanying. Before I could stop myself, I yelled, "Brent, I could just KILL you!"

At that moment, Brent's face was filled with fear and horror. His image and reply still haunt me. With his eyes brimming with tears and his arms extended, Brent whispered, "Oh Mama! Does that mean I have to go on the cross?"

Brent's only concept of death and dying was the cross that Jesus died on. To this day, I have not forgotten the pain I caused with my thoughtless, hasty, and cruel words. I prayed to my merciful Father and asked him to forgive me for my behavior. I am so appreciative of the unlimited second chances he has given me.

Brent is now 22 and living in a city far from home. In a phone conversation not long ago I shared a distressing issue I was having with a mutual friend. As he heard the pitch of my voice rise, he interrupted me respectfully and reminded me of the verse I had used to counsel him over the years. "Mom, remember what Proverbs 15:1 says? 'A gentle answer turns away wrath.' Maybe you ought to consider that right now. You know, it worked for us when we tried it."

Thank you, Brent. Lesson heeded.

Mom, My Heart Needs Mending

PRAISE GOD THAT HE IS THE COMFORTER

Praise be to the God and Father of our Lord Jesus Christ,
the Father of compassion and the God of all comfort,
who comforts us in all our troubles.

2 CORINTHIANS 1:3–4

Praise be to the God of all comfort. May he be exalted above all nations. Heavenly Father, what a blessing your comfort is in my life, always available, freely given, and endless in its supply. You feel every hurt and save every tear. You are never absent from my affliction, but are always ready to console, soothe, calm, reassure, and heal. Praise the Lord of heaven and earth for he is a God of sweet, gentle comfort.

CONTINUED PRAISE

God comforts those who mourn (MATTHEW 5:4).
Praise God for his compassion for the afflicted (ISAIAH 49:13).
Praise God for the Holy Spirit who is our personal comforter
(JOHN 14:16, 26).
We can find comfort and healing through his Word (Psalm 119:50).

144

CONFESSION

O my Comforter in sorrow,
my heart is faint within me.

JEREMIAH 8:18

Dear Lord, I am going through a very painful time. I feel like I'm drowning in my own tears. I have asked you to remove the situation and yet nothing has changed. I feel alone and uncomforted. I have accused you of not caring and being absent from my life. Forgive me for these accusations, for I know deep in my heart they are not true. Wash away my tears and enable me by faith to feel the comfort of your arms wrapped tightly around me.

REFLECTION: Think of other times that God has helped you get through difficulties in your life. God listens and will bring to your heart the comfort you need.

Repeat these truths over and over until they bring peace to your soul:

God is close to the brokenhearted (PSALM 34:18).
God is always with me (JOSHUA 1:9).
God cares about me (1 PETER 5:7).
God comforts just as a mother comforts her child (ISAIAH 66:13).

Thanksgiving

When anxiety was great within me,
Your consolation brought joy to my soul, O LORD.
Psalm 94:19

Heavenly Father, thank you for giving me such sweet comfort when I am worried, lonely, weary and discouraged. I thank you for the Bible — my greatest source of comfort. Your words console my spirit and bring joy back to my heart. When my heart is filled with pain, I am so grateful that there is never a shortage of your comforting grace at those times in my life. I cherish your comfort that brings calmness to my storms, restoring my hope. Thank you also for the times you have brought me comfort through the call or visit of a friend at just the right moment.

Continued Thanks

Think of all the ways God has changed your heart since you came to Jesus. Thank God for the work he has done in your life. Give thanks for God's promises of comfort...

When you are discouraged (LAMENTATIONS 3:20–23; ROMANS 8:28–29).
When you are weary (MATTHEW 11:28–30; PHILIPPIANS 4:12–13).
When you feel lonely (ISAIAH 49:14–16; JOHN 14:15–21).
When you feel anxious (MATTHEW 6:25–27; PHILIPPIANS 4:4–7).

INTERCESSION

The LORD has sent me to bind up the brokenhearted …
to bestow on them a crown of beauty instead of ashes, the oil of gladness
instead of mourning, and a garment of praise instead of a spirit of despair.

ISAIAH 61:1, 3

My Father, I ask you to bind up my child's broken heart. Please grant him a crown of beauty instead of ashes, the oil of gladness instead of mourning, and a garment of praise instead of a spirit of despair. My heart aches to see my child carrying around hurts and frustrations that I can't fix. I wish I could. Only you, Jesus, can heal him. Only you can mend a heart that has been trampled. He needs your healing touch. Wipe away his tears and bring back a song of joy to his life. Turn my child's despair into praise. Let him experience your unfailing love so he can trust in your all-wise and perfect plan for his life. For your honor and glory I pray in the name of Jesus, Amen.

CONTINUED INTERCESSION

Pray that by faith your child will know God's presence is with him (ISAIAH 43:2).
Pray that he will experience God's loving support and comfort
(PSALM 94:18–19; ISAIAH 49:13).
Pray that he seeks God's Word and the Holy Spirit for comfort
(PSALM 23:4; LUKE 11:13).
Pray that he runs to God in times of suffering (PROVERBS 18:10;
MATTHEW 11:28–30).

GOD'S PROMISE FOR YOUR CHILD

The LORD is close to the brokenhearted and saves those who are crushed in spirit.

PSALM 34:18

LIFE HAPPENS

In high school, my son was diligent and driven with one goal in mind: being accepted at an Ivy League school. His GPA was high; his SAT scores were exceptional; and his extracurricular portfolio was extensive. He had a clear vision of the goal ahead and what it would take to get there.

That is why the entire family went into a state of shock when he didn't get into an Ivy League school. As parents, we were confused and puzzled. Tim was devastated.

I took a very heavy heart to prayer group that week. My prayer partners who had prayed weekly with me asked God to put Tim in the college environment for which he was destined, and this brought comfort to me.

A few weeks before he was to leave for college, Tim opened one of his sealed transcripts and discovered a typographical error. With hurricane fury he bolted into my study and tossed the transcript on my lap. His face was fire-engine red with rage. Mine was white with disbelief. How could this have happened? We were both overcome with anger, distress, helplessness, and feelings of rejection.

Leaving Tim at the "school of his misfortune" was the most difficult goodbye of our lives as parents. As we drove away, my husband was silent. I was praying, "Lord, heal Tim's heart. Show him your plans for this turn in his life, and that these plans are for your glory and Tim's good.

God heard my prayers and his answer has been astonishing, above and beyond anything I could have imagined. Tim is thriving at school, academically, spiritually, and relationally. He is experiencing a new and vital relationship with God and a restored hunger for the Word. He is active in Bible study, involved in dorm life, and always on the front row of dorm debates and discussions about spiritual topics.

Life is what happens, but Tim is seeing life through a different lens these days. He sees that when God is in charge, what happens is the best plan of all. My son is living out his destiny in the place of God's choosing.

Mom, I Need a Caring Spirit

PRAISE GOD FOR HE IS COMPASSIONATE

The LORD is gracious and righteous;
our God is full of compassion.

PSALM 116:5

Almighty King, I worship you for being a God of infinite, matchless compassion. You empathize with and enter into our suffering, and bring healing and wholeness. Your compassion is like a mother having compassion on her children — you have a gracious heart, full of mercy and forgiveness. And because of Jesus, you enable me to be compassionate as well. With joyful lips I declare that your compassions never fail—they are new every morning. Great is your faithfulness.

CONTINUED PRAISE

God's compassion never fails (LAMENTATIONS 3:22–23).
God's compassion is great (PSALM 119:156; NEHEMIAH 9:19).
God shows compassion to those in distress (ISAIAH 49:13).
God's anger is restrained because of his compassion (JOEL 2:13; JONAH 3:10).

CONFESSION

Have mercy on me, O God,
according to your unfailing love;
according to your great compassion
blot out my transgressions.

PSALM 51:1

Dear Lord, many times I have been moved to tears because I was emotionally stirred by a sad situation and yet I did nothing to help. Jesus, I want to have a compassionate heart like you, a heart that is moved to act in response to the suffering I see. May compassion begin in my own home. Forgive me for the times I ignore my family's hurts. Help me to stop, listen, and tenderly care for my family with a compassionate heart.

REFLECTION: Have there been times that you have knowingly turned the other way when you saw someone in need? Jesus wants us to portray his compassionate heart to the world. Ask him to reveal ways you can model it.

Thanksgiving

When Jesus saw the crowds, he had compassion on them,
because they were harassed and helpless,
like sheep with out a shepherd.

Matthew 9:36

Thank you Jesus, for being the embodiment of God's compassion. There is nothing that I go through that you do not understand or care about. Thank you for being such an incredible example of compassion. Matthew 15 tells a story of your caring compassion. "Great crowds came to him, bringing the lame, the blind, the crippled, the mute and many others, and laid them at his feet; and he healed them." Jesus, you personally met the needs of the people who came to you. I am so grateful your compassion was not in word only, but also in deed. I rejoice with great thankfulness that I can count on your never- failing compassion in my life.

Continued Thanks

Thank God for the ways in which you have personally benefited from Jesus' compassion. What has he delivered you from? Helped you through? Comforted you in? Expect his compassion today.

INTERCESSION

As God's chosen people, holy and dearly loved, clothe yourselves with compassion, kindness, humility, gentleness and patience.

COLOSSIANS 3:12

Dear Jesus, please help my child decide to clothe himself with compassion, kindness, humility, gentleness and patience. May he seize opportunities to be caring and kind toward others. I pray that he will not be so self absorbed that he overlooks the hurting and the wounded around him. Motivate him toward compassionate actions that will make a difference in his little corner of the world. May he serve others with a heart of compassion. In Jesus' name, Amen.

CONTINUED INTERCESSION

Pray for your child to experience the Father's compassion (PSALM 103:13).
Pray that he loves others with his actions (1 JOHN 3:17–18).
Pray that he will identify with the needs of those around him (HEBREWS 13:1–3).

GOD'S PROMISE TO YOUR CHILD

*If you spend yourselves in behalf of the hungry
and satisfy the needs of the oppressed,
then your light will rise in the darkness,
and your night will become like the noonday.*

ISAIAH 58:10

DONUTS ANYONE?

There we were—running late on a Sunday morning. Again! My husband dressed five-year-old Blake while I pulled a jumper over 2-year-old Abby's blond curls. Minutes later we pulled out of the driveway. I was still applying last-minute make-up as we made the turn into the church parking lot.

On a horizon full of happy, noisy little people, I noticed a scene that puzzled me. Two children were selling donuts three feet away from the backdoor of the church. I looked around expecting to spot some supervising parents, but found no one. Blake interrupted my train of thought with his question— "What are they doing, Mom?"

"Selling donuts, son."

He looked wistfully at the sugar-studded treats. "Can we buy some?"

"No, sweetie," I replied. "But I'll give the kids some money anyway." I handed some coins to the children. Their faces beamed—ours beamed back. It felt good to help these little strangers.

When we finally settled into our seats in the worship center, I sensed the nudging of the Spirit, and I listened. I remembered when the Lord had scolded His own disciples for not bringing the children to Him.

After the service I hurried to Blake's classroom and found him in the center of a huddle of kindergartners and teacher's aides. Blake asked, "Mom, where are the donut girls? Are they still here? We need to talk to them." My twinkle-eyed son had come up with a plan that was simple but efficient. Everyone would come to church early next week, buy up all the donuts, and invite these girls to Sunday School. "See, those girls get to hear about Jesus and God and the Bible while we all have donuts. And maybe they'd bring their mom and dad."

The compassionate resolution in Blake's voice stunned me. I breathed a silent prayer, thanking God for this display of childlike faith. Blake had compassionately and effortlessly expressed the heart of God—serving others with childlike simplicity.

That day was like most other Sunday mornings— bustle and buzz. But two wide-eyed little salespeople and one determined little boy reminded me what the Master said so many years ago. "I love the little children. Let them come."

Mom, I Need Freedom from My Fears

Praise God Because He is the Deliverer

The Lord is my light and my salvation—
whom shall I fear?
For in the day of trouble
he will keep me safe in his dwelling;
he will hide me in the shelter of his tabernacle
and set me high upon a rock.
Psalm 27: 1, 5

I exalt you Eternal God, my mighty deliverer. Because of your great love you deliver me from all my fears. Sovereign Lord, nothing is too hard for you. You reach down from heaven to deliver and rescue me from suffering, trouble, and distress. You delight to save your loved ones from the hand of the enemy. I praise you that your deliverance is sure and you are faithful. Hallelujah!

Continued Praise

God rescues us from the dominion of darkness (Colossians 1:13).
God delivers us from our troubles (Psalm 34:17; Psalm 41:1–2).
God delivers us from the wrath to come (1 Thessalonians 1:10).

154

CONFESSION

Help us, O God our Savior,
for the glory of your name,
deliver us and forgive our sins
for your name's sake.

PSALM 79:9

My Lord, forgive me for holding onto my fears. I often feel anxious for my children. I worry that they will not follow your ways and they will do things that could be destructive to themselves as well as others. Lord, set me free from an anxious mind. Help me to trust you. You delight in rescuing me, and you are able to deliver me from all my fears. Help my unbelief and turn my fear to faith.

REFLECTION: Identify your fears. Tell them to the Lord and ask him to help you trust rather than be afraid. Replace your anxious thoughts with this promise:

There is no fear in love; perfect love drives out all fear.
So then, love has not been made perfect in anyone who is afraid,
because fear has to do with punishment.

1 JOHN 4:18 GNT

Thanksgiving

This is what the Lord says, …
"Fear not, for I have redeemed you;
I have summoned you by name; you are mine.
When you pass through the waters, I will be with you;
and when you pass through the rivers,
they will not sweep over you."

ISAIAH 43:1–2

Father, for all eternity I will sing of the security only you can provide. I rest secure in the knowledge that when you called me by name, you made me yours. No matter where the trials of my life take me, you will deliver me safely. I need not fear anything. I rejoice that you are able to rescue me from any situation that might cause my family or me harm. Thank you for the promise that you will be my deliverer today as well as in all my tomorrows.

Continued Thanks

Reflect on the times God saved you from evil, danger or set you free from your fears. Tell your children of his amazing deliverance. Encourage them to put their fears in God's strong arms.

INTERCESSION

I sought the LORD, and he answered me; he delivered me from all my fears.
Those who look to him are radiant; their faces are never covered with shame.

PSALM 34:4–5

My Father, I ask that this will be said of my child: that she sought the Lord,
and you answered her and delivered her from all her fears. May her face be
radiant and unashamed because she looks to you for reassurance. Help her to
know that you are able to deliver her from all her fears — that your perfect
love casts out fear. Help my child to rely on the power of the Holy Spirit to
provide the courage and faith she needs to go forward. May she replace her
fears with the promises of your Word. In Jesus' name, Amen.

CONTINUED INTERCESSION

Pray that she experiences God's deliverance from evil
(MATTHEW 6:13; 2 THESSALONIANS 3:2).
Pray for your child to be delivered from all her troubles (PSALM 34:19).
Pray that she memorizes the promises of God concerning fear (ISAIAH 41:10;
PSALM 27:1; PSALM 91:11–12; HEBREWS 13:6; PSALM 46:1–2; PSALM 32:7).

GOD'S PROMISE FOR YOUR CHILD

God did not give us as spirit of timidity,
but a spirit of power, of love and of self-discipline.

2 TIMOTHY 1:7

Batter, Up!

At age seven, Virginia had her doubts about softball. She had never tried it before. All the kids were older. She couldn't catch a ball and she was sure she couldn't hit a ball. What if the ball hit her? Her list of worries grew each time the subject came up.

But as her mom, I had some insights of my own. I knew this was just a little creek of fear. Virginia would have much bigger rivers to cross, and I was certain that this was a relatively safe risk for her. She might enjoy it and even have fun! With that in mind, I signed her up.

Hours before the first practice I found Virginia curled in a sad little ball. "Mom, don't make me do this," she cried. "I can't hit that ball … and everyone's going to laugh at me."

I sat down on the edge of her bed and tenderly rubbed her back, which was vibrating with each new sob, and told her the tale of another frightened rookie.

"Honey, do you remember the story of Moses?" I asked. "Remember when God told him to go to Pharaoh? Moses felt just like you; he was scared. He told God, 'I can't speak. Even if I could, he won't listen. Can't you find somebody else?'"

I began to detect a little glow of courage building as my daughter listened to one of her favorite Bible stories. Her response warmed my heart. "Mom, can we just pray for a minute?"

We clasped hands and asked God to go to practice with Virginia and show her what to do and how to do it, just like he did for his servant Moses.

By the time softball season ended, my little slugger had become an avid softball enthusiast. She may not be the rookie of the year, but she crossed her creek of fear and barely got her feet wet.

Moses and Virginia both tried something they had never attempted before. Both were convinced that God had picked the wrong person for the task. But when they asked for help, God came through, for both of them. Doesn't he always?

Mom, I Want to be Like Jesus

PRAISE GOD BECAUSE HE IS HOLY

Each of the four living creatures had six wings and was covered with eyes all around, even under his wings. Day and night they never stop saying:

> *"Holy, holy, holy*
> *is the Lord God Almighty,*
> *who was, and is, and is to come."*

REVELATION 4:8

Heavenly Father, holy is your name. I worship you in the splendor and beauty of your holiness. I marvel that your divine holiness is the essence of your very nature, that your holiness is the foundation of all your other attributes; wisdom, love, and power are all holy. There is none holy beside you. "Praise the LORD. . . praise his holy name" (Psalm 103:1).

CONTINUED PRAISE

God is majestic and holy (EXODUS 15:11; ISAIAH 6:1–3; PSALM 99:3).
God's holiness is manifested in all his ways and his works (PSALM 145:17–18).
God's holiness is manifested in his Word (ROMANS 7:12).

Confession

Whatever is true, whatever is noble,
whatever is right, whatever is pure,
whatever is lovely, whatever is admirable—
if anything is excellent or praiseworthy—
think about such things.

PHILIPPIANS 4:8

My Holy Lord, please forgive me for letting my thoughts
and actions go to things that are unlovely and impure.
I desire the beauty and freedom that holiness brings.
Set me free from those things that prevent me
from bringing honor to your holy name.
I want the beauty of Christ's holiness flowing in and through me.

REFLECTION: Ask the Holy Spirit to search your heart and reveal anything that may be keeping you from being radiant for Jesus. If you confess and repent, see what God promises he will do:

Blessed are the pure in heart,
for they will see God.

MATTHEW 5:8

Thanksgiving

God has reconciled you by Christ's physical body
through death to present you holy in his sight,
without blemish and free from accusation.

COLOSSIANS 1:22

My Jesus, I love you.
I rejoice greatly that you were the perfect holy, sacrifice.
With a thankful heart I rejoice that you purchased my salvation—
taking my place on the cross. You took on my sin and in exchange
poured your goodness and righteousness into me.
You have given me the Holy Spirit to transform me into your likeness.
I look forward to the day you will present me before the Father Righteous.
What a glorious gift. With tears of joy I contemplate so great a love.

CONTINUED THANKS

Let the truth of Jesus' words penetrate deep into your heart:
You did not choose me, but I chose you and appointed you to go
and bear fruit—fruit that will last.

JOHN 15:16

Intercession

We, who with unveiled faces all reflect the Lord's glory,
are being transformed into his likeness with ever-increasing glory,
which comes from the Lord, who is the Spirit.

2 Corinthians 3:18

Dear Jesus, I pray that my child will be transformed into your likeness with ever-increasing glory, which comes from the Lord, who is the spirit. I know he has been set him apart to live a life worthy of you, bearing fruit in every good work. May his heart's desire be to please you. May he love the things you love. When he is tempted I ask that he will draw on the strength and power of the Holy Spirit to help him do what is right. Jesus, I pray my child will grow up to be just like you. In Jesus name, Amen.

Continued Intercession

Ask God to fill your child with the Holy Spirit (Ephesians 5:18).
Pray for your child to seek God above all else (Psalm 27:4; 42:1).
Pray that your child lives a life pleasing to God (1Thessalonians 4:3–8).

God's Promise for Your Child

Dear friends, now we are children of God,
and what we will be has not yet been made known.
But we know that when he appears, we shall be like him,
for we shall see him as he is.

1 John 3:2

LUNCH MONEY

It has long been my prayer that my children will have hearts that do not allow them to do things that break the heart of God and they grow up to act like Jesus. Last year, I saw the answer to my prayers begin to emerge in my oldest son.

As a senior in high school, Dan was the captain of the varsity baseball team and self-absorbed in himself, a common condition of teens. One afternoon during spring practice, he stumbled into the kitchen and doubled over with sobs. Alarmed to see my usually self-sufficient senior in this state, I mentally reviewed possible scenarios: a car wreck, a friendship clash, a failed exam, or maybe an injury sustained during practice. Dan pulled out a chair and motioned me to sit. Wiping the tears from his face with his sleeve, his emotions began to settle down.

I could feel my own tears welling up as Dan began to share with me. That afternoon during baseball practice, Dan had heard the cry of God's heart and felt God's pain for Shaun, one of his very lost teammates. Overcome with grief, Dan ended up running to the field house to hide his tears.

"Mom, I couldn't look at Shaun without crying," Dan told me. "He needs Jesus so bad, and it's breaking my heart."

By then we were both crying as Dan continued his story. He had been buying Shaun's lunch all year and had cut a deal with his friend: Come to church with me and the debt is cancelled.

Dan's pitch worked. The following Sunday, Dan and Shaun sat together in church. I saw a scene I had only dreamed about— my strapping son, maturing and influencing others and growing to be like his Savior. I liked the change. It suited Dan well.

a Note From Fern

I would like to personally invite you
to join a Moms In Touch group
or start one for the mothers in your area.
Women in Moms In Touch love God and their children,
and are committed to prayer and standing together
on the promises of God's Word.
As you unite with mothers in prayer,
you will receive the hope that God gives
and see the power of his work in the lives of your children.

To find a group in your area or to obtain information about
Moms In Touch and how to start a group, please call:

1-800-949-MOMS

ACKNOWLEDGEMENTS

Heavenly Father, I give you all the honor and glory for giving me the Holy Spirit's wisdom and guidance in writing this book. Your unfailing love and patience was my source of confidence. I pray that this book will bring countless women to an intimate relationship with the Beloved and give them courage to join other moms in prayer. Grant them the faith to trust you with the very lives of their children.

To my husband Rle, our children, Ty, Troy, Travis, Trisha, and their wives Patti, Bonnie and Tara. Thank you for your prayers and your sweet encouragements.

My sincere thanks to you, my dear friend, Connie Kennemer for writing and compiling the stories. You made the journey of writing this gift book a joy. God gave us unforgettable memories of precious prayer times, laughter, tears and collaboration around my kitchen table. I am profoundly grateful to the Lord for connecting our lives through Moms In Touch so many years ago.

Ann Spangler, you will never know how much your faith in me carried me through the "what in the world am I doing" times. Thank you for believing in me and for all your initial help. Caroline Blauwkamp, I marvel that you never once doubted the book's inception or its completion. Nancy Kennedy, I am so grateful God brought you in on the project to edit both Connie's and my work. Your kind encouragement was just what we needed to give us the confidence we needed. Janice Jacobson, thank you for never once making me feel like I couldn't do it. You have the patience of Job.

To my book intercessor prayer team, MITI headquarters staff and Leadership, this is our book. Words cannot adequately express my sincere gratitude for all the prayers you offered on my behalf. This book is definitely the result of your prayers.

"Every hard duty that lies in your path, that you would rather not do, that it will cost you pain and struggle or sore effort to do, has a blessing in it. Not to do it, at whatever cost, is to miss the blessing."

L.B. COWMAN

Thank you Father, that you did not let me miss the blessing.

*The stories in this book are
from praying mothers in Moms In Touch groups.
I thank each of you for your creativity, your story,
and your prayers. I love you all!*

*Jodie Berndt, Sally Burke, Marlae Gritter,
Jill Hanes, Julie Herzog, Julie Heying, Nancy Kennedy,
Connie Kennemer, Christine LaFata, Nancy Lindgren,
Martha Little, Jennifer Martin, Sue Mooney, Jan Peck,
Andrea Robertson, and Jan Shockey.*

*I would also like to thank my son Troy
for his contribution as a child
who was prayed for by a Moms In Touch group.*

Also Available from Inspirio:

MOM'S PRAYERS FROM THE HEART
A Guided Journal
by Fern Nichols

PRAYERS FROM A GRANDMA'S HEART
Asking God's Blessing and Protection
for all Your Grandchildren
by Quin Sherrer

GRANDMA'S PRAYERS FROM THE HEART
A Guided Journal

PRAYERS FROM A DAD'S HEART
Asking God's Blessing and Protection for Your Children
by Robert Wogemuth

DAD'S PRAYERS FROM THE HEART
A Guided Journal

Let this be written for a future generation,

that a people not yet created may praise the LORD...

PSALM 102:18

_____

_____

_____

_____

_____

_____

_____

_____

_____